D0369528

TALES FROM
THE VIENNA WOODS

Tales from
the Vienna Woods

Ödön von Horváth

translated by

CHRISTOPHER HAMPTON

FABER & FABER

London · Boston

First published in 1977
by Faber and Faber Limited
3 Queen Square London WC1
Reprinted 1978
Printed in Great Britain by
Whitstable Litho Whitstable
All rights reserved

ISBN O 571 11063 O

CHARACTERS

ALFRED

ALFRED's MOTHER

ALFRED's GRANDMOTHER

FERDINAND VON HIERLINGER

VALERIE

OSKAR

IDA

HAVLITSCHEK

THE CAPTAIN

A LADY

MARIANNE

ZAUBERKÖNIG

TWO AUNTS

ERICH

EMMA

HELENE

THE SERVANT

THE BARONESS

THE CONFESSOR

THE AMERICAN

THE COMPÈRE

The action of the play takes place in 1931, in Vienna,
in the Vienna Woods and in the Wachau region outside
Vienna.

The first production of *Tales From The Vienna Woods* in
this translation was given at the National Theatre early
in 1977.

'Nothing gives as strong an impression
of infinity as stupidity.'

English translations of the songs in the text appear at the end of the book.

INTRODUCTION

On June 1st, 1938, Ödön von Horváth left his Paris hotel
for a meeting with Robert Siodmak, the film producer; they
were to discuss the possibility of making a film based on
Horváth's novel *Jugend Ohne Gott*. Afterwards, as far as
can be established, Horváth went, alone, to a cinema on
the Champs Elysées to see Walt Disney's *Snow White and the
Seven Dwarfs*. He had made arrangements to meet his friends
Hertha Pauli and Carl Frucht that evening in their usual
bistro. At about 7.30, he was walking down the Champs
Elysées, when a storm of unusual violence arose. He
crossed the street and joined a group of people sheltering
under a chestnut tree opposite the Théâtre Marigny. As the
storm continued, an adjacent elm collapsed on to the chestnut tree, causing a branch to break off. It struck Horváth
on the back of the head, killing him instantly. No-one
else was hurt. He was the author of seventeen plays (not
counting sketches, fragments and rewrites), three novels
and other miscellaneous pieces. He was 36.

It was in 1931 that Horváth, at any rate in terms of
critical success and public recognition, reached the peak
of his career. In that year he was awarded the Kleist
prize, then the most prestigious of German literary

1

awards, by Carl Zuckmayer, himself, along with Brecht and
Robert Musil, a former winner of the prize. The Nazi press
was incensed by the spectacle of Zuckmayer ('the half-Jew')
awarding a German prize to Horváth ('the young Hungarian'):
as well it might have been since Horváth's play *Italienische
Nacht (Italian Night)* had attacked and derided the Nazis
even more mercilessly than Zuckmayer's *Captain of Köpenich*.
'The German proposes and the Jew disposes,' the *Völkischer
Beobachter* declared mysteriously in the course of a typically frenzied attack on the award.

And it was in 1931, in November, that Horváth's play
*Geschichten aus dem Wiener Wald (Tales From The Vienna
Woods)* had its premiere at the Deutsches Theater, Berlin,
directed by Heinz Hilpert, with Peter Lorre as Alfred and
Carola Neher as Marianne. It was an immediate success and
has remained the most popular and often-performed of his
plays; but even so, the minority who booed and hissed at
the first night were a reminder of how fragile was the
position in which at that time the most talented German
writers found themselves.

His father was a Hungarian diplomat and his childhood
was spent in the various cities in which his father was
posted. He was fourteen, he said, before he wrote a
sentence in German. Nevertheless, he thought of himself,
and felt it necessary, in those racially-conscious times,
to stress this in interviews, as a German writer, although
he retained his Hungarian passport. 'I'm a typically
Austro-Hungarian affair,' he said.

Tales From The Vienna Woods, like *Italian Night,* which
preceded it, and *Kasimir und Karoline,* which followed, was
described by Horváth as a *Volksstück,* a term it would not

be particularly meaningful to translate, as, essentially, it was a critical renovation of a tradition we are not familiar with, that of the nineteenth-century Austrian comedies of Nestroy and Raimund. In fact these three plays, generally regarded as Horváth's masterpieces, evolved a style as personal to Horváth as so-called 'epic theatre' was to Brecht. 'More a descriptive form than a dramatic form', Horváth said, and his purpose was nothing less than to describe, in large-scale, but carefully constructed plays, the decay of a society haunted by inflation (an earlier play, *Sladek*, was sub-titled 'a history from the age of inflation') and lurching towards Fascism. Horváth, unlike Brecht, was not a didactic writer, asking on the one hand for a cool, detached audience and on the other hand presenting them with an open-and-shut case; and indeed, if you look at the earlier drafts and scenes eventually not included in *Tales From The Vienna Woods*, it is clear that Horváth drew back from anything that might seem too crudely oversimplified. The interplay between individual selfishness and the pressures of a society in crisis is impartially portrayed, and only the liveliness and compassion with which each individual character, even the most reprehensible, is drawn, show where Horváth's sympathies lay. All these plays deal with losers in what Horváth called 'the gigantic battle between the individual and society' and behind them lies a powerful sense of people who have been through bad times and have still worse to come.

Worse came. Horváth's next play *Glaube Liebe Hoffnung (Faith Hope and Charity)*, a more intimate, small-scale piece than the preceding three plays, went into rehearsal in 1933. It never opened. Shortly afterwards, his

3

parents' house in Murnau was ransacked by the SA, and
Horváth set off into the half-life of exile. For the next
five years he travelled almost continuously, sometimes
venturing back into Germany, while his newest plays remained either unperformed or received matinée performances
in Vienna or German-language performances in Prague. His
work became harsher and darker and he ventured into new
areas with two plays which used familiar figures as a
means to examine the themes of exile and the breakdown of
society, *Figaro Lässt Sich Scheiden (Figaro Gets a Divorce)*
and *Don Juan Kommt Aus Dem Krieg (Don Juan Comes Back From
the War)*, the latter perhaps the strongest and most des-
pairing play he wrote. Finally, whether exasperated by
the pointlessness of writing plays which were unlikely to
be satisfactorily performed, or gripped by a new inspira-
tion, he turned back to the novel, a form he had used only
once before. The result was *Jugend Ohne Gott (Youth
Without God)*, a brilliant study of the Hitlerjugend, which
was an immediate success and was translated into several
languages. He followed this up with *Ein Kind Unserer
Zeit (A Child of Our Time)*, working frenziedly now, and
announcing, soon after it was finished, that he was going
to start on another novel, *Adieu Europa*. He left Vienna
on the 13th March, 1938, just in time, as it turned out,
and the next two months, as his exile began in earnest,
were like some speeded-up parody of his childhood: Prague,
Budapest, Trieste, Venice, Milan, Zurich, Brussels and
Amsterdam. Eventually, on the 28th May, he arrived in
Paris.

After Horváth's bizarre and sensational death, his
name passed into obscurity for about twenty years. Then,
towards the end of the fifties, his plays gradually began

to reappear in the repertoire of German theatres, and what came to be known as the 'Horváth Renaissance' slowly gathered momentum, until, in the 1970-71 season, there were twenty-five major productions of Horváth's plays in German-speaking theatres. Even more significantly, a number of young playwrights, including Franz Xaver Kroetz, Martin Sperr and Wolfgang Bauer, declared their allegiance to Horváth, and he replaced Brecht as the central influence on new German and Austrian plays. Peter Handke, as well, writing in 1968 on Horváth, took the opportunity to launch a broadside against Brecht, contrasting his simple solutions 'which for me are nothing more than a *bon mot* or an aphorism', with the much richer texture and far more ambiguous effects of Horváth, who has the ability, 'elsewhere only to be found in Chekhov or Shakespeare', to write a line, often banal in intself, but so dislocating, as to suggest and contain an infinite variety of response.

When I began work on this translation, I received a number of amiable messages, more or less implying that the project was impossible. Horváth's use of language was so personal, *Tales From The Vienna Woods* so local in its atmosphere, that any attempt to convey the flavour of the play in English was unlikely to succeed. The fact that none of Horváth's plays (with the curious exception of *Sladek*, broadcast on Radio 3 in 1970) have been performed in English, to my knowledge, was not simply a reflection of the notorious insularity of the English-speaking theatre; there were other reasons, to wit, the man's work was simply untranslatable. To begin with, there was the problem of the dialect. Then there was Horváth's individual use of the dialect. And so on.

All this is true: and this, although it is as accurate

as I can make it, does not pretend to be a scholarly translation of the play. I have not attempted to find an equivalent English dialect, because in England (as is not the case in Vienna) dialect is inextricably connected with class, and the result would have been inevitably misleading. I was fortified in this decision by Horváth's own remarks in his *Gebrauchsanweisung (Instructions)*, written reluctantly as a result of his dissatisfaction with a number of productions of his plays. In the course of this document he lists a number of 'director's deadly sins', the first of which starts as follows: '1. Dialect. Not a word to be spoken in dialect! Every word must be spoken in good German *(hochdeutsch)*, at any rate as if spoken by someone who normally only speaks in dialect, and is now forcing himself to speak good German. This is very important!' I have therefore chosen a neutral language, differentiated, of course, from character to character, but flexible enough, I hope, to conform to Horváth's enigmatic (and occasionally contradictory) instructions.

Sean O'Casey would have been a wonderful translator of Horváth: and an Irish writer might well have been able to provide a more colourful version of some of Horváth's more eccentric turns of phrase than I have managed. But this is only a beginning for a great and original writer, who has much to say to us, that is both narrowly relevant (and I write on a day when the pound has fallen seven cents against the dollar) and perennially true.

I should like to thank Ian Huish and Maximilian Schell, who have both worked patiently through the text with me, pointing out errors and making valuable suggestions. Their purpose throughout was to bring me closer to Horváth, and any distance that still remains is my fault, not theirs.

In 1971, an indignant reader wrote to the *Rheinische*

Post to complain about the misleading title of *Tales From The Vienna Woods*. This deliberate irony on Horváth's part, this violent contrast between the cliché Vienna (Strauss waltzes and old imperial bonhomie) and the stark and bitter reality had deceived and enraged him. The letter ended: 'No-one should blame Johann Strauss. He was not in a position to protect his title. His waltzes travelled all over the world. Horváth's miserable series of everyday episodes will scarcely achieve that.'

I believe it will.

Horváth was a deeply superstitious man: and in a time when fear at what was happening in Europe was widespread among intellectuals, Horváth suffered from a number of more (apparently) irrational fears. 'There are worse things than the Nazis,' he once said, 'for example, the things one is afraid of without knowing why.'

In Amsterdam, the week before his death, Horváth visited a clairvoyant (male or female, accounts differ). In any event, the clairvoyant became extremely excited and told him that he must go to Paris, it was absolutely essential, because the greatest adventure of his life awaited him there. As we know, he took the advice.

Almost exactly a year before his death, Horváth was talking to his friend Franz Theodor Csokor, explaining to him why he, Horváth, tried never to go out at the end of May or the beginning of June, because of his conviction that he would die an accidental death on one of those dates. In the course of that conversation, he said something which, apart from its uncanny prophetic quality, seems to me to illuminate the strange atmosphere which clings to even the most ordinary exchanges in *Tales From The Vienna Woods*. He said: 'Why is it most people are

afraid of the darkness of the forest? Why aren't they
afraid of walking down the street?'

                                        Christopher Hampton

Act One

OUT IN THE WACHAU

The entrance to a cottage at the foot of a ruined castle.
ALFRED sits in the open air, tucking into bread and butter
and curds. His MOTHER is just bringing him a sharper
knife. There's a humming and ringing in the air, as if
the dying strains of Johann Strauss's waltz Tales From The
Vienna Woods *were being played somewhere over and over*
again. And the beautiful blue Danube is not far off.
ALFRED's MOTHER watches him. Suddenly she grips his hand,
the one holding the knife, and looks deep into his eyes.
ALFRED, startled, stares at her suspiciously, his mouth
full of food. Silence. She strokes his hair, slowly.

MOTHER: It's sweet of you, Alfred dear ... I'm so glad
    you haven't completely forgotten your poor old mother,
    dear ...
ALFRED: What do you mean, completely forgotten you? I
    would've come out ages ago, if I could've managed it.
    But nowadays, what with the depression and everyone
    rushing about, you can't get anything done. If my
    friend Ferdinand von Hierlinger hadn't brought me out
    in his convertible, who's to say when you'd've seen me.
MOTHER: I'm sure it's very thoughtful of your friend, Herr
    von Hierlinger.

9

ALFRED: Yes, well, he's kindness itself. He's coming to
fetch me in half an hour or so.

MOTHER: Already?

ALFRED: Afraid so.

MOTHER: Don't eat all the curds then, otherwise I'll have
nothing to offer him ...

ALFRED: He doesn't want curds, Hierlinger, he's not allowed
them anyway, he's got chronic nicotine poisoning. He's
a proper businessman, very well thought of. I see a
great deal of him.

MOTHER: On business?

ALFRED: Among other things.

(Silence.)

MOTHER: Are you still with the bank?

ALFRED: No.

MOTHER: Why not?

(Silence.)

ALFRED: The bank's no use to me, you got no opportunities,
it's a dead end. Work in the old sense, it's just not
worth the candle. Nowadays, if you want to get
on, what you have to do is use other people's work.
I'm on my own now. Handling money, that kind of
thing . . .

*(He chokes and coughs violently. His MOTHER slaps
him on the back.)*

MOTHER: Isn't it nice?

ALFRED: Yes, but I practically choked.

MOTHER: I'm glad it's nice, anyway.

(Silence.)

ALFRED: Speaking of choking, where's Granny?

MOTHER: I think she's in the kitchen, praying.

ALFRED: Praying?

MOTHER: Well, she's been worrying a lot lately.

10

ALFRED: Worrying?

   (*Silence.*)

MOTHER: Don't forget her birthday, whatever you do. She's
   eighty next month, and if you forget her birthday,
   we'll have hell again. You are her favourite, you
   know.

ALFRED: I'll make a note of it. (*He makes a note of it.*)
   Granny's birthday. Eighty. (*He gets up, full.*)
   What you might call a biblical age. (*He looks at his
   watch.*) Nearly time for Hierlinger, I think. He
   should be here any minute. He'll have a lady with
   him.

MOTHER: What sort of a lady?

ALFRED: Oldish.

   (*Silence.*)

MOTHER: How old?

ALFRED: Middle-aged, you know.

MOTHER: Rich?

ALFRED: How should I know?

   (*Silence.*)

MOTHER: Nothing wrong with money. It's just you've never
   found the right girl.

ALFRED: Maybe. Sometimes I think I'd like to have a few
   kids around me, but then I think, well, if it's not
   to be ...

   (*ALFRED's GRANDMOTHER comes out of the cottage,
   carrying her bowl of curds.*)

GRANDMOTHER: Frieda! Frieda!

MOTHER: Where's the fire?

GRANDMOTHER: Who's stolen my curds?

MOTHER: Me. Our Alfred was still hungry.

   (*Silence.*)

GRANDMOTHER: Oh, he was, was he? Nobody bothers to ask

me. I might just as well be dead. *(To ALFRED's MOTHER.)* That'd suit you, wouldn't it?

(ALFRED sticks his tongue out at her.)

ALFRED: Yah!

(Silence. Then she sticks her tongue out at ALFRED.)

GRANDMOTHER: Yah!

(Silence.)

GRANDMOTHER *(shrieking)*: I don't want it anyway! So there!

(She throws away the contents of the bowl. FERDINAND VON HIERLINGER enters with VALERIE, carefully made-up, fiftyish, wearing a motoring outfit.)

ALFRED: May I introduce you? This is my mother and this is my friend Ferdinand Hierlinger. Frau Valerie ... and over there is my dear old granny.

MOTHER: It's very kind of you, Herr von Hierlinger, to bring Alfred out to see me, thank you, thank you very much ...

HIERLINGER: Oh, please, it's nothing. Alfred knows I'll be only too happy to bring him out here whenever he likes, he only has to say the word.

MOTHER: Does he?

HIERLINGER: Of course ...

(He stops, realising he has somehow blundered. Embarrassed silence.)

VALERIE: It's so beautiful out here ...

MOTHER: Perhaps they'd like to have a look round the tower?

HIERLINGER: What tower?

MOTHER: Ours. Up there.

HIERLINGER: You mean to say those lovely romantic ruins are yours?

MOTHER: No, they belong to the State. We just look after

12

them. But I'd be delighted to show you round if you
like. If you climb up to the top you'll be rewarded
with a magnificent view and a most instructive
panorama.

HIERLINGER: Too kind, dear lady, I'd love to, love to.

MOTHER *(smiling, embarrassed)*: It'll be a pleasure.

(To VALERIE.) And perhaps you'd erm ...

VALERIE: No, no thanks, I'm so sorry, but the height, you
know, I can never get my breath.

MOTHER: Well, we shan't be long.

(She exits with FERDINAND VON HIERLINGER.)

VALERIE *(to ALFRED)*: Would you mind just helping me out
on a point of information?

ALFRED: What's your problem?

*(ALFRED's GRANDMOTHER sits at the table, tries
unsuccessfully to eavesdrop.)*

VALERIE: You've been cheating me again.

ALFRED: Will that be all?

VALERIE: Hierlinger tells me the pay-out on the last race
at Saint-Cloud was not 168 schillings, it was 222
schillings.

ALFRED: Hierlinger's lying.

VALERIE: And the paper, I suppose that's lying too?

*(She waves a racing newspaper under his nose.
Silence.)*

(Triumphantly) Well?

ALFRED: You're not a fair woman, do you know that? This
kind of thing, you're just driving me away from you.

VALERIE: Now perhaps you'll be so kind as to pay me what
you owe me. 27 schillings. S'il vous plaît.

(ALFRED gives her the money.)

ALFRED: Voilà!

VALERIE: Merci.

13

(She counts it.)

ALFRED: You are a mean-minded individual.

VALERIE: I am not an individual. And from now on I shall
have to insist on a written receipt, whenever you ...

ALFRED *(interrupting her)*: Oh, do stop rabbitting on,
will you?

(Silence.)

VALERIE: I wish you wouldn't cheat me all the time,
Alfred ...

ALFRED: And I wish you wouldn't be so suspicious all
the time, it's just ruining our arrangement. You
have to take into account the fact there's light
and shade in any young man, it's only natural. And
just one word in your ear: any personal relationship, the only thing makes it work is when there's
something in it for both of you. All the rest is
rubbish. So, you're right, there's no reason to
break off a friendly business relationship, just
because the other's not doing us any good ...

VALERIE *(interrupting him)*: I never said that,
I ...

ALFRED: There you go, you see, changing your tune again.
You're very frivolous, you know, you really are, not
to mention arrogant. I take a Civil Service widow's
pension and what do I do with it? I use a bit of nous,
I know a bit about horses, and because of my lucky
touch, instead of a Civil Service widow's pension,
you're drawing the same salary as the full-time head
of some government department. Now what's the matter?

VALERIE: I was just thinking about the grave.

ALFRED: What grave?

VALERIE: His grave. I can't help it, whenever I hear the
words Civil Service, I think about his grave. *(Pause.)*

14

I don't do nearly enough to look after it. My God, I
should think it's all overgrown ...

ALFRED: Listen, Valerie, if I win tomorrow at Maisons-
Laffitte, we'll have his grave completely overhauled.
We'll go halves.

(VALERIE suddenly kisses his hand.)

ALFRED: Get off ...

HIERLINGER *(off)*: Alfred! Alfred! It's beautiful up here.
I'm on my way down.

ALFRED *(calling up to him)*: Ready! *(He stares at
VALERIE.)* Are you crying?

VALERIE *(tearfully)*: Of course not ... *(She looks at
herself in her mirror.)* God, I'm a mess ... time I
shaved again.

*(She puts on some more lipstick and hums Chopin's
Funeral March.)*

GRANDMOTHER: Alfred!

(ALFRED goes over to her.)

When are you coming again? Soon?

ALFRED: Sure.

GRANDMOTHER: I don't like goodbyes, you know. As long as
nothing happens to you, I can't help worrying ...

ALFRED: What's going to happen to me?

(Silence.)

GRANDMOTHER: When am I going to get my money back?

ALFRED: Soon as I have it.

GRANDMOTHER: Thing is, I need it.

ALFRED: What do you need money for?

GRANDMOTHER: I'm eighty next month, and when I'm buried, I
want it paid for with my own money, I don't want
charity, you know what I'm like ...

ALFRED: Don't you worry about it, Granny.

QUIET STREET IN VIENNA 8

From left to right: OSKAR's superior butcher's shop,
with sides of beef and veal, sausages, hams and boars'
heads on display. Next to it a dolls' hospital, under the
sign 'Zum Zauberkönig', with jokes and novelties, death's
heads, dolls, toys, tin soldiers and a skeleton in the
window. Finally, a small tobacconist's with newspapers,
periodicals and picture postcards in front of the door.
Above the dolls' hospital, a balcony with flowers, part
of the ZAUBERKÖNIG's flat.
OSKAR stands in the doorway of his shop in his white
apron, cleaning his fingernails with a penknife. Every
now and then he stops to listen, for on the second floor
someone is playing Tales From The Vienna Woods by Johann
Strauss on a clapped-out piano.
IDA, a bright, thin, short-sighted eleven-year-old, comes
out of the butcher's with her shopping-bag, and is on her
way out, right, when she stops in front of the dolls'
hospital and looks in the window.
HAVLITSCHEK, OSKAR's assistant, a huge man with bloody
hands and an equally bloody apron, appears in the doorway
of the butcher's. He is devouring a sausage and he's
furious.

HAVLITSCHEK: Stupid bitch, stupid ...
OSKAR: Who?

    (HAVLITSCHEK points at IDA with his long knife.)
HAVLITSCHEK: That one. Told me my blood-sausage was off,
    didn't she, stupid little bitch. My God, for two pins
    I'd stick her and watch her running round with the knife
    in her throat, like that pig yesterday, that'd be a laugh.

OSKAR *(smiles)*: You think so?

> *(IDA senses OSKAR's gaze, and it frightens her. All of a sudden she runs off, right. HAVLITSCHEK laughs. The CAPTAIN enters, left. He's been pensioned off since the end of the war, and is in civilian clothes. He nods to OSKAR. OSKAR and HAVLITSCHEK bow: and the waltz comes to an end.)*

CAPTAIN: Well, I really must say, that blood-sausage yesterday. My compliments. First class.

OSKAR: Tender, wasn't it?

CAPTAIN: A poem.

OSKAR: Hear that, Havlitschek?

CAPTAIN: Oh, is he the one we have to ...?

HAVLITSCHEK: Ready for inspection, captain.

CAPTAIN: My respects.

HAVLITSCHEK: You're a real connoisseur, captain, sir. A gourmand. A man of the world.

CAPTAIN *(to OSKAR)*: I've been transferred to just about every corner of our old monarchy in my time, but what I always say is, standards. That's what counts. Standards.

OSKAR: It's all a question of tradition, captain.

CAPTAIN: If your poor dear mother had been spared, she'd have been very proud of her son.

OSKAR *(smiles, flattered)*: Well, it just wasn't to be, captain.

CAPTAIN: Yes, we all have to go some time.

OSKAR: She's been gone a year today.

CAPTAIN: Who?

OSKAR: My mama.   After lunch, about half past two. That's when Our Lord released her from her troubles.
> *(Silence.)*

CAPTAIN: Is it a year already?

17

(Silence.)

OSKAR: If you'll excuse me, captain, I have to go and get
spruced up. For the requiem mass.

(He exits.

No reaction from the CAPTAIN, who is elsewhere.

Silence.)

CAPTAIN: Another year gone. Pace till twenty, trot till
forty, and then comes the gallop.

(Silence.)

HAVLITSCHEK *(eating again)*: Beautiful funeral they give
the old lady.

CAPTAIN: Yes, it was a great success.

*(He leaves him standing there and crosses to the
tobacconist's, pausing for a moment to look at the
skeleton in the window of the dolls' hospital. Upstairs, someone starts playing again, this time the
waltz* Über den Wellen.

*HAVLITSCHEK watches the CAPTAIN's progress, then spits
out the sausage-skin and goes back into the butcher's.*

VALERIE appears in the doorway of her tobacconist's.

The CAPTAIN greets her and she responds.)

CAPTAIN: May I have a look at the lottery results?

*(VALERIE gets them from the rack by the door and
hands them to him.)*

Enchanté.

*(He buries himself in the list of results. The waltz
suddenly breaks off, in mid-phrase.)*

VALERIE *(maliciously)*: And what have we won, then, captain?
The big prize?

(The CAPTAIN hands her back the list.)

CAPTAIN: I've never yet won anything, Frau Valerie.
Goodness knows why the devil I bother. The most I've
ever managed is to win my stake back.

18

VALERIE: Well, lucky in love ...

CAPTAIN: Long ago, long ago.

VALERIE: Come on, captain, with your profile?

CAPTAIN: If you're a choosy sort of a chap, I'm afraid
that has very little to do with it. And it can be
expensive, if your character's that way inclined. If
the war had only lasted a fortnight longer, I'd be
drawing a major's pension today.

VALERIE: If the war had lasted a fortnight longer, we'd
have won.

CAPTAIN: As far as one can tell.

VALERIE: There's no doubt about it.

(She exits into her shop.
MARIANNE shows a LADY out of the dolls' hospital.
Every time the shop door opens, there's a peal of
bells. The CAPTAIN leafs through a newspaper and
eavesdrops.)

LADY: I can rely on you, then, can I?

MARIANNE: Absolutely, madam. This is the best and oldest
shop in the whole district. And we specialise in tin
soldiers. They're guaranteed and we always deliver
on time.

LADY: I'll go over it again, shall I, just to make sure
everything's clear. That's three boxes of seriously
wounded and two boxes of dead. And cavalry as well,
please, not just infantry. And you will be sure to
deliver them early the day after tomorrow, otherwise
there'll be tears from the little one. It's his
birthday on Friday, and he's been wanting to play
doctor for ages ...

MARIANNE: They're guaranteed and we always deliver on
time, madam. Thank you very much, madam.

LADY: Well, goodbye then.

(She exits, left.

The ZAUBERKÖNIG appears on his balcony in his dressing-gown. His moustaches are still taped.)

ZAUBERKÖNIG: Marianne? Where are you?

MARIANNE: Papa?

ZAUBERKÖNIG: Where have you hidden my suspenders?

MARIANNE: The pink ones or the beige ones?

ZAUBERKÖNIG: There's only the pink ones left.

MARIANNE: They're in your chest of drawers, top left-hand drawer, right-hand side at the back.

ZAUBERKÖNIG: Top left-hand drawer, right-hand side at the back. Difficile est, satiram non scribere.

(He disappears.)

CAPTAIN *(to MARIANNE)*: Always on the go, Fräulein Marianne. Always on the go.

MARIANNE: Nothing wrong with hard work, captain.

CAPTAIN: Far from it. By the way, when will our congratulations be in order?

MARIANNE: What for?

CAPTAIN: Well, your engagement.

(The ZAUBERKÖNIG reappears on the balcony.)

ZAUBERKÖNIG: Marianne!

CAPTAIN: Good morning to you, Herr Zauberkönig.

ZAUBERKÖNIG: Good morning to you, captain. Look, Marianne, for the last time, where are my suspenders?

MARIANNE: Where they always are.

ZAUBERKÖNIG: Now what sort of an answer is that, I ask you? And a very nice tone of voice, I must say. Is that the way to speak to your father? Wherever it is they always are, they aren't there.

MARIANNE: Then they're in the cupboard.

ZAUBERKÖNIG: No.

MARIANNE: Then they're in your bedside cabinet.

20

ZAUBERKÖNIG: No.

MARIANNE: Then they're in with your underpants.

ZAUBERKÖNIG: No.

MARIANNE: Then I don't know where they are.

ZAUBERKÖNIG: I'm asking you once and for all: where are my suspenders?

MARIANNE: I don't know, I'm not a magician!

ZAUBERKÖNIG: *(yells at her)*: And I'm not going to the requiem mass with my socks round my ankles! Just because you're sloppy with my clothes! Now come up here and look for them! Come on, avanti, avanti!

(MARIANNE exits into the dolls' hospital. As she does so, the waltz Uber den Wellen *starts up again. The ZAUBERKÖNIG listens.)*

CAPTAIN: Who's that playing?

ZAUBERKÖNIG: She's a schoolgirl. Lives on the second floor. Talented child, she is.

CAPTAIN: Musical.

ZAUBERKÖNIG: Precocious.

(He hums the tune, sniffs the flowers, enjoying their scent.)

CAPTAIN: Spring soon, Herr Zauberkönig.

ZAUBERKÖNIG: It's taken long enough! Even the-weather's gone mad.

CAPTAIN: Like everyone else.

ZAUBERKÖNIG: Not me. *(Pause.)* It's a miserable time, though, captain, miserable. You can't even afford a servant any more. If I didn't have my daughter ...

(OSKAR comes out of the butcher's, dressed in black and wearing a top hat. He is pulling on a pair of black kid gloves.)

I shan't keep you a minute, Oskar. It's Marianne. She's lost my suspenders again, thanks to her magic touch.

CAPTAIN: Perhaps you'll permit me to offer you my suspenders, Herr Zauberkönig. I've taken to wearing garters as well, this last ...

ZAUBERKÖNIG: How very kind of you, enchanté, but we must have order. Marianne will just have to use her magic touch to find them again.

CAPTAIN: May I congratulate the prospective bridegroom?

(OSKAR lifts his hat and bows slightly.)

ZAUBERKÖNIG: God willing.

CAPTAIN: Good day, gentlemen.

(He exits, and the waltz ends. MARIANNE steps on to the balcony with the pink suspenders.)

MARIANNE: Here we are, I've found your suspenders.

ZAUBERKÖNIG: About time.

MARIANNE: You threw them in the linen basket by mistake. I had to go poking through all the dirty washing.

ZAUBERKÖNIG: Well well well. *(He smiles paternally and pinches her cheek.)* Clever girl. Oskar's down there.

(He exits.)

OSKAR: Marianne! Marianne!

MARIANNE: Yes?

OSKAR: Aren't you coming down?

MARIANNE: I've got to anyway.

(She exits. HAVLITSCHEK appears in the doorway of the butcher's, eating again.)

HAVLITSCHEK: I wanted to ask you, Herr Oskar. Say an Our Father for me, will you, please, for your poor old mother?

OSKAR: I'd be glad to, Havlitschek.

HAVLITSCHEK: Thanks.

(He exits. MARIANNE comes out of the dolls' hospital.)

OSKAR: I'm very happy, Marianne. It's almost over now,
   my year of mourning, and tomorrow I won't have to wear
   my crape any more. And the engagement's announced
   on Sunday, and we'll get married at Christmas. Give
   us a kiss, Marianne, just a little good morning
   kiss.

   (MARIANNE kisses him, then pulls away suddenly.)
MARIANNE: Ow! Why d'you always have to bite?
OSKAR: Did I?
MARIANNE: Don't you even know when you're doing it?
OSKAR: I could have sworn ...
MARIANNE: Why d'you always have to hurt me?

   (Silence.)
OSKAR: Cross?

   (Silence.)

   Are you?
MARIANNE: Sometimes I think what you really want in your
   heart of hearts is for me to behave really badly.
OSKAR: Marianne! You know how religious I am. I take my
   Christian principles very seriously.

MARIANNE: I suppose you think I'm an atheist, do you? Huh!
OSKAR: I didn't mean to insult you. I know you despise me.
MARIANNE: You are an idiot, what are you talking about?

   (Silence.)

OSKAR: Don't you love me, then?
MARIANNE: Love, what is it?

   (Silence.)

OSKAR: What are you thinking about?
MARIANNE: Oskar, if there's anyone going to make us split
   up, it's you. You mustn't keep pestering me about
   what I'm thinking, please ...
OSKAR: I wish I could see inside your head. I wish I
   could get inside your skull and find out what you're

thinking in there.

MARIANNE: Well, you can't.

OSKAR: Man is an island.

>*(Silence. OSKAR fetches a bag of sweets out of his
>pocket.)*

>Would you like a sweet, I forgot I had them, the ones
>in gold paper are liqueur.

>*(MARIANNE sticks a large sweet in her mouth, mechani-
>cally. The ZAUBERKÖNIG hurries out of his shop, also
>wearing black and a top hat.)*

ZAUBERKÖNIG: Well, here we are then. What's that you've
>got there? Sweets again? Well, that's very kind,
>very kind indeed. *(He puts one in his mouth.)*
>Pineapple! Delicious! Well, what have you got to say
>to your fiancé, then? Happy?

>*(MARIANNE exits quickly into the dolls' hospital.)*

ZAUBERKÖNIG *(surprised)*: What's the matter with her, then?

OSKAR: Bad mood.

ZAUBERKÖNIG: Sauce! She doesn't know when she's well off.

OSKAR: Come on, it's getting late, Papa, the mass ...

ZAUBERKÖNIG: That's no way to behave. I hope you're not
>spoiling her. Don't do that, Oskar, whatever you do.
>You'll suffer for it if you do. What do you think I
>had to put up with in my marriage? And not because
>my lady wife was a bad-tempered old hag, God bless
>her, but because I could never bring myself to do any-
>thing dishonourable. Never let go of your authority.
>Keep your distance. Remember, it's a patriarchy, not
>a matriarchy. So, chin up and thumbs down! Ave
>Caesar, morituri te salutant!

>*(He exits with OSKAR.*

>*Upstairs, the schoolgirl starts playing Ziehrer's
>waltz In* lauschiger Nacht.

MARIANNE appears in the window, re-arranging the
display. She takes particular trouble with the
skeleton.
ALFRED enters, left, catches sight of MARIANNE's back,
stops and watches her. MARIANNE turns, sees ALFRED
and looks at him with some fascination. ALFRED
smiles. MARIANNE smiles back. ALFRED bows, charmingly.
MARIANNE acknowledges him. ALFRED approaches the
window. VALERIE is standing in the doorway of her shop,
watching ALFRED. ALFRED drums on the window. MARIANNE
looks at him, suddenly frightened, and pulls the blind
down quickly. The waltz breaks off, in mid-phrase.
ALFRED notices VALERIE. Silence.)

VALERIE: And where are you off to?

ALFRED: To see you, darling.

VALERIE: Lost something, have we?

ALFRED: I thought I might buy you a dolly.

VALERIE: And to think I pinned all my hopes on a creature like you.

ALFRED: Sorry, I'm sure.

(Silence. ALFRED chucks VALERIE under the chin.
VALERIE slaps his hand. Silence.)

ALFRED: Who's that girl, then?

VALERIE: None of your bloody business.

ALFRED: Very pretty girl, is that.

VALERIE: Ha!

ALFRED: Fine figure of a girl. How come I've never seen
her before? That's what I call a cruel twist of fate.

VALERIE: Do you?

ALFRED: Now, listen, you, I'm not going to put up with
your hysterical jealousy much longer. I don't let
anyone push me around, that's something I can very
well do without.

VALERIE: Oh, can you?

25

ALFRED: And don't think I give a damn about your money.
  (Silence.)
VALERIE: Yes, that would be best, I think ...
ALFRED: What would?
VALERIE: It would be best not to see each other any
  more.
ALFRED: Well, about bloody time! I should think so. I've
  been waiting for that. There you are. That's what I
  owe you. With your receipt. We broke even at Saint-
  Cloud and we won at Le Tremblay. Outsiders. You'd
  better check it!
  *(He exits. VALERIE, alone, counts the money mechani-
  cally. Then, a lingering look after ALFRED.)*
VALERIE *(quietly)*: Bastard. Shit. Pimp. Pig.

III

THE FOLLOWING SUNDAY IN THE VIENNA WOODS

*A clearing on the bank of the beautiful blue Danube. The
ZAUBERKÖNIG, MARIANNE, OSKAR, VALERIE, ALFRED, various
distant relatives, including ERICH from Kassel in Prussia,
and a number of ugly little children dressed in white are
having a picnic. All of them are grouped artistically,
waiting to be photographed by OSKAR, who at the moment is
fiddling with his tripod. Then he gets into position
next to MARIANNE and triggers the automatic release.
It all works perfectly and the group dissolves in move-
ment.*

ZAUBERKÖNIG: Wait! Again! Da capo! I think I
  moved.
OSKAR: But Papa!

ZAUBERKÖNIG: Better safe than sorry.

FIRST AUNT: That's right.

SECOND AUNT: Otherwise you'll always regret it.

ZAUBERKÖNIG: Come on, da capo, da capo!

OSKAR: Oh, all right, then.

(He busies himself with his equipment, and once again the automatic release works perfectly.)

ZAUBERKÖNIG: That's better.

(The group gradually disperses.)

FIRST AUNT: Herr Oskar, will you do me an enormous favour? Will you just take a picture of the little ones on their own, they look so sweet today.

OSKAR: Yes, of course, with pleasure.

(He arranges the children in a group, kissing the smallest one.)

SECOND AUNT *(to MARIANNE)*: Just look how good he is with the children. If he wouldn't make a wonderful father, I don't know who would. He worships children, he just worships them. Oh, well, touch wood, eh?

(She embraces MARIANNE and kisses her.)

VALERIE *(to ALFRED)*: Well, this is the last straw.

ALFRED: Whatever do you mean?

VALERIE: Tagging on to these people when you knew I'd be here. After everything that's passed between us.

ALFRED: What do you mean, what's passed between us? We've just split up, that's all. Doesn't mean we're not still good friends.

VALERIE: It's obvious you're not a woman. Otherwise you might have some respect for my feelings.

ALFRED: What feelings? I thought they'd changed.

VALERIE: It's not so easy for a woman to forget. There's always something inside that stays the same. Even if you are just a big swindler.

ALFRED: Look, be reasonable, will you?

VALERIE (*suddenly full of animosity*): Yes, that'd just
    suit you, wouldn't it?

    (*Silence.*)

ALFRED: May the swindler be excused now, please?

VALERIE: Who invited you today?

ALFRED: I'm not saying.

VALERIE: Not too difficult to guess, though, is it?

    (*ALFRED lights a cigarette.*)

    Where did we get to know each other, then? In the
    toyshop?

ALFRED: Shut up.

    (*The ZAUBERKÖNIG approaches ALFRED with ERICH.*)

ZAUBERKÖNIG: I understand you gentlemen haven't met. May
    I introduce my nephew Erich, my wife's brother-in-
    law's son by his second marriage. And this is Herr
    Zentner. That's right, isn't it?

ALFRED: Yes.

ZAUBERKÖNIG: Herr von Zentner.

    (*ERICH has a haversack and a canteen on his belt.*)

ERICH: Very pleased to meet you.

ZAUBERKÖNIG: Erich is a student. From Dessau.

ERICH: Kassel, Uncle.

ZAUBERKÖNIG: Kassel, Dessau, always mix them up.

    (*He moves away.*)

ALFRED (*to VALERIE*): Do you know each other?

VALERIE: We've known each other for ages.

ERICH: We met just recently. We had a discussion about
    the Burgtheater and all this nonsense about the
    triumph of the sound film.

ALFRED: How interesting.

    (*He bows formally and moves away. One of the AUNTS
    puts a record of* Your Tiny Hand is Frozen *on her*

portable gramophone.)

ERICH *(listening)*: *La Bohème.* Divine Puccini.

   (MARIANNE, now next to ALFRED, also listens.)

MARIANNE: Your tiny hand is frozen ...

ALFRED: It's *La Bohème.*

MARIANNE: Puccini.

VALERIE *(to ERICH)*: What's your favourite operetta?

ERICH: Operettas have nothing to do with art.

VALERIE: Go on, how can you say a thing like that?

ERICH: Have you read *The Brothers Karamazov*?

VALERIE: No.

ERICH: That's art.

MARIANNE *(to ALFRED)*: I always wanted to study eurhythmics,
   my ambition was to run my own institute, but my family
   aren't interested in anything like that. Papa always
   says, when a woman's financially independent from a
   man, it's the last step on the road to Bolshevism.

ALFRED: I don't know much about politics, but I'll tell
   you this: when a man's financially dependent on a
   woman, that's not so wonderful, either. Laws of
   nature, I suppose.

MARIANNE: I don't believe that.

   *(OSKAR is taking photographs of the ZAUBERKÖNIG on
   his own, in various poses. The music has stopped.)*

ALFRED: Keen on photography, is he, your fiancé?

MARIANNE: He's obsessed with it. We've known each other
   for eight years.

ALFRED: How old were you when you met? I'm sorry, that
   just slipped out automatically.

MARIANNE: I was fourteen.

ALFRED: Not very old.

MARIANNE: I suppose we were childhood friends. He was
   the boy next door.

29

ALFRED: What if he hadn't been the boy next door?

MARIANNE: What do you mean?

ALFRED: I mean, I suppose it's all the laws of nature.
And fate.

(Silence.)

MARIANNE: Fate, yes. I mean, I don't think it's really
what people call love, at least, it may be as far as
he's concerned, but ... as far as ... *(she suddenly catches
ALFRED's eye.)* No, what am I saying, I hardly know
you ... God, you certainly know how to drag it all out
of a person ...

ALFRED: I'm not trying to drag anything out of you. That's
the last thing I want to do.

MARIANNE: You must be a hypnotist.

OSKAR *(to ALFRED)*: Excuse me. *(To MARIANNE.)* May I?
*(He gives her his arm and leads her towards a beauti-
ful group of old trees, beneath which everyone else
has already settled down for a picnic. ALFRED follows
OSKAR and MARIANNE and, like them, sits down.)*

ZAUBERKÖNIG: Now what was it we were talking about?

FIRST AUNT: The transmigration of souls.

SECOND AUNT: Transmigration of souls, what's that when it's
at home?

ERICH: It's a Buddhist idea. Part of their religious
philosophy. The Buddhists maintain that the soul of
a dead man passes into an animal: an elephant, say.

ZAUBERKÖNIG: Ridiculous.

ERICH: Or a snake.

FIRST AUNT: Disgusting!

ERICH: What's disgusting about it? That's just another of
our petty human prejudices. We ought to acknowledge
the secret beauty of the spider, the beetle and the
centipede ...

30

SECOND AUNT (*interrupting him*): Not just before tea, if
    you don't mind.
FIRST AUNT: I feel quite peculiar.
ZAUBERKÖNIG: Nothing's going to spoil my appetite today.
    I don't believe in all those creepy-crawlies.
VALERIE: Stop it!
    (*The ZAUBERKÖNIG rises and taps his glass with his
    knife.*)
ZAUBERKÖNIG: Dear friends! Latterly it's become an open
    secret that my dear daughter Marianne has looked
    favourably on dear Oskar ...
VALERIE: Bravo!
ZAUBERKÖNIG: Just a minute, I shan't be much longer, and
    now we've all gathered here, that's to say, I've
    invited you all here, to celebrate simply but with
    dignity, in a small but select circle, a very impor-
    tant moment in the lives of these two, now in the flower
    of their youth. My only deep regret today is that
    Almighty God has not spared Marianne's dear precious
    mother, God rest her soul, my unforgettable wife, to
    share this day of joy with her only daughter. But I'm
    sure of one thing, she's somewhere up there now in
    Heaven, standing behind a star and looking down on
    us. And raising her glass ... (*He raises his glass.*)
    ... in a heartfelt toast to the happy and hereby
    officially engaged couple. Three cheers for the young
    couple, Oskar and Marianne, hip hip ...
ALL: Hooray!
ZAUBERKÖNIG: Hip, hip ...
ALL: Hooray!
ZAUBERKÖNIG: Hip, hip ...
ALL: Hooray!
    (*IDA, the bright, thin, short-sighted little girl who*

31

complained about HAVLITSCHEK's blood-sausage, steps
forward in front of the engaged couple, dressed in
white, holding a bouquet, and recites. She has a
speech defect.)

IDA: Love is a very precious stone,

It burns for ever, all alone

And never fades away.

It burns as long as Heaven's light

Transfigured in Man's eyes so bright,

Dawns with each passing day.

(Cheers and cries of 'How sweet!'. etc., as IDA hands
MARIANNE the bouquet with a curtsey. Then everyone
caresses IDA and congratulates the happy couple in the
highest of spirits. The portable gramophone strikes
up with the Wedding March, and the ZAUBERKÖNIG kisses
MARIANNE on the forehead and OSKAR on the mouth. Then
he wipes the tears from his eyes and lies down in his
hammock. Meanwhile, ERICH and OSKAR have drunk a
toast of friendship from ERICH's canteen.)

ERICH: Ladies and gentlemen, your attention, please! Oskar
and Marianne! I'm going to take the liberty of drinking
a very special toast to you from my canteen here. Good
luck, good health and a lot of good upstanding German
children! Cheers!

VALERIE *(tipsy)*: And no niggers, eh? Cheers!

Sieg Heil!

ERICH: Excuse me, Madame, but I'm afraid this is one subject
on which I cannot allow frivolous remarks. As far as
I'm concerned the subject is sacred. You know my
position vis-à-vis our racial problems.

VALERIE: Problems, problems. Wait, don't go away, you
difficult man, you ...

ERICH: Difficult. What do you mean?

32

VALERIE: Interesting ...

ERICH: In what way?

VALERIE: You think I like the Jews?   You big
     baby ...
     (She links arms with the big baby and drags him off.
     Everyone settles down in the wood, and the little
     children play and do their best to disturb them.
     OSKAR plays the lute and sings.)

OSKAR: Sei gepriesen, du lauschige Nacht,

     Hast zwei Herzen so glücklich gemacht.

     Und die Rosen im folgenden Jahr

     Sahn ein Paar am Altar!

     Auch der Klapperstorch blieb nicht lang aus,

     Brachte klappernd den Segen ins Haus.

     Und entschwand auch der liebliche Mai,

     In der Jugend erblüht er neu!

     (He plays the song through again, humming instead of
     singing. Everyone else, except for ALFRED and
     MARIANNE, joins in, humming along with him.
     ALFRED approaches MARIANNE.)

ALFRED: May I congratulate you again?

     (MARIANNE closes her eyes. ALFRED gives her hand a
     lingering kiss. OSKAR has been watching, has handed
     his lute to the SECOND AUNT, crept over to them and
     now stands next to MARIANNE.)

     (Formally) Congratulations.

OSKAR: Thank you.

     (ALFRED bows formally and moves away. OSKAR watches
     him go.)

OSKAR: He's jealous of me. He's got no manners. Who is
     he, anyway?

MARIANNE: A customer.

OSKAR: Since when?

33

MARIANNE: He came in yesterday, and we talked for a bit, not for long, and I invited him. He bought a game.

VALERIE *(shrilly)*: I have a forfeit, what's my forfeit?

ERICH: It's you have to moo three times.

VALERIE: Auntie Henriette, you're it, Auntie Henriette.

(The FIRST AUNT strikes a pose and bellows.)

FIRST AUNT: Moo! Moo! Moo!

(Loud laughter.)

VALERIE: And I have a forfeit, what's my forfeit?

ZAUBERKÖNIG: You have to baa three times.

VALERIE: Well, you're it.

ZAUBERKÖNIG: Baa! Baa! Baa!

(Howls of laughter.)

VALERIE: And I have a forfeit, what's my forfeit?

SECOND AUNT: It's you have to give a demonstration.

ERICH: What of?

SECOND AUNT: Whatever you can.

VALERIE: Oskar! Hear that, Oskar? You have to give us a demonstration.

ERICH: Anything you like.

ZAUBERKÖNIG: Whatever you can do.

(Silence.)

OSKAR: Ladies and gentlemen, I'm going to give you a demonstration of something really useful. I've been studying the Japanese method of self-defence. What they call ju-jitsu. Now, pay attention, please, this is the easiest way to disarm your opponent.

(He suddenly lunges at MARIANNE and demonstrates his hold on her, throwing her to the ground.)

MARIANNE: Ow! Ow! Ow!

FIRST AUNT: Don't be so rough.

ZAUBERKÖNIG: Bravo! Bravissimo!

OSKAR *(to the FIRST AUNT)*: It was only a pretend throw,

34

otherwise I could have damaged her spine.

FIRST AUNT: Well, that's nice, isn't it?

ZAUBERKÖNIG *(slapping OSKAR on the back)*: Very clever!
Very well illustrated!

SECOND AUNT *(helping MARIANNE up)*: You're such a delicate
plant. Well, now, have you another forfeit?

VALERIE: Afraid not. All gone. That's the lot.

ZAUBERKÖNIG: Then I have a suggestion. Let's all go for a
swim. In the river, it'll be nice and cool. I'm
sweating like a boiled monkey.

ERICH: Excellent idea.

VALERIE: But where are the ladies going to change?

ZAUBERKÖNIG: Nothing could be simpler. Ladies to the
right, gentlemen to the left. And we'll meet again in
the beautiful blue Danube.

(The portable gramophone is playing The Blue Danube
Waltz *and the ladies disappear to the right, the
gentlemen to the left. VALERIE and ALFRED are the
last to leave.)*

VALERIE: Alfred.

ALFRED: Yes?

*(VALERIE hums along with the waltz tune and takes her
blouse off.)*

What?

(VALERIE throws him a kiss.)

Goodbye.

VALERIE: Wait a minute. What does the young sir think of
the bride to be?

*(ALFRED looks at her, then goes up to her quickly and
stops just in front of her.)*

ALFRED: Breathe out.

VALERIE: Whatever for?

ALFRED: Breathe out!

35

(VALERIE breathes on him.)

ALFRED: Old soak!

VALERIE: Just a bit merry, that's all, what are you, a
vegetarian? Man proposes and God disposes. It's not
every day there's an engagement party ... or is it a
disengagement party, you swine?

ALFRED: There's no need to take that tone.

VALERIE: Don't you touch me, don't you dare lay a finger
on me!

ALFRED: When have I ever laid a finger on you?

VALERIE: The seventeenth of March.

(Silence.)

ALFRED: Well, you have got a memory, haven't you?

VALERIE: I remember everything. Good and bad. *(She
suddenly holds the blouse up in front of her.)* Now
go away, I want to get undressed!

ALFRED: Well, that wouldn't be much of a surprise for me,
would it?

VALERIE *(shrieking)*: Stop staring at me. Go away! Go
away!

ALFRED: Hysterical cow.

(He exits, left. VALERIE, alone, watches him go.)

VALERIE: Bastard. Shit. Rat. Pig.

*(She undresses. The ZAUBERKÖNIG emerges from behind
the bushes in his swimsuit and watches her. VALERIE,
now only in slip, underwear and stockings, notices
him.)*

VALERIE: Jesus, Mary and Joseph! Oo, you wicked creature!
Peeping Tom, that's what you are.

ZAUBERKÖNIG: Now, now, I'm not a pervert. Don't worry
about me, just carry on undressing.

VALERIE: I do have my modesty, you know.

ZAUBERKÖNIG: Go on, nobody worries about that sort of

36

thing these days.

VALERIE: Yes, I know, but I have such a vivid imagination ...

*(She skips behind a bush. The ZAUBERKÖNIG sits down
in front of the bush, finds VALERIE's corset, picks
it up and sniffs it.)*

ZAUBERKÖNIG: Imagination or no imagination, these days,
it seems to me, the world's going mad. No loyalty,
no beliefs, no moral principles. Everything's
collapsing, nothing's certain any more. Ready for the
Flood. *(He lays the corset aside, the smell is ob-
viously nothing to write home about.)* I'm just happy
to have settled Marianne, you can always rely on a
butcher's shop.

VALERIE: What about a tobacconist's?

ZAUBERKÖNIG: Oh, yes. Smoking, eating, there'll
always be a demand for that ... but magic?
When I think about the future, I get very pessi-
mistic sometimes. I haven't had it easy in
my life, not at all easy, you've only got to
think of my dear wife, all that endless bother with
the specialists ...

*(VALERIE appears in a woollen bathing costume, fiddling
with her straps.)*

VALERIE: What did she actually die of?

ZAUBERKÖNIG *(staring at her bosom)*: Breasts.

VALERIE: Not cancer?

ZAUBERKÖNIG: That's right. Cancer.

VALERIE: Poor thing.

ZAUBERKÖNIG: Well, it wasn't very nice for me, either.
The left one, she had to have off. She never was very
healthy, but of course her parents never told me.
When I look at you, though, by comparison: imposing,

I'd go as far as to say regal. A regal figure.

(VALERIE touches her toes a few times.)

VALERIE: You men, what do you know about the tragedy of
women? If we didn't spend all our time doing ourselves up and taking care of our appearances ...

ZAUBERKÖNIG *(interrupting her)*: Don't you think I have to
take care of my appearance?

VALERIE: Of course. But with a man it's the inner
qualities you look for first.

*(She does a bit of eurhythmics. The ZAUBERKÖNIG
watches her and starts doing knee-bends.)*

VALERIE: That's enough, I'm worn out.

(She throws herself down next to him.)

ZAUBERKÖNIG: The dying swan.

(He sits down next to her. Silence.)

VALERIE: May I rest my head in your lap?

ZAUBERKÖNIG: In the garden there is no sin.

VALERIE *(doing so)*: It's still very hard, the earth ...
it's been such a long winter.

(Silence.)

(Softly) You. How do you feel? When the sun shines
on my skin like this, I always get so, I don't know ...

ZAUBERKÖNIG: So ... what?

(Silence.)

VALERIE: I saw you playing with my corset just now.

(Silence.)

ZAUBERKÖNIG: What about it?

VALERIE: What about it?

*(The ZAUBERKÖNIG suddenly throws himself on her and
kisses her.)*

My God, you're so impetuous. I never would have
thought it of you ... you naughty man, you ...

ZAUBERKÖNIG: Am I naughty? Am I naughty?

VALERIE: Yes ... no, you're ... stop it, someone's coming!
   (They roll apart. ERICH enters in a swimming costume
   with an air-gun.)
ERICH: Excuse me, Uncle. Do you mind if I do some
   shooting?
ZAUBERKÖNIG: What do you want to do?
ERICH: Shoot.
ZAUBERKÖNIG: You want to shoot? Here?
ERICH: Yes, at the target on that beech over there. The
   monthly competition of our student cadet corps is the
   day after tomorrow, and I just thought I'd get in some
   practice, if you don't mind. May I?
VALERIE: Of course.
ZAUBERKÖNIG: Of course? *(To VALERIE.)* Of course! *(He*
   gets up.) The cadet corps. Oh, yes, of course! You
   mustn't forget how to shoot, whatever you do. Per-
   sonally, I'm going to get cooled down. In the beautiful blue Danube. *(Aside.)* Hang yourselves, all I care.
   (He exits. ERICH loads, aims and fires. VALERIE
   watches him, speaks after the third shot.)
VALERIE: Excuse me, I don't mean to interfere with you,
   but what is it you're studying at the moment?
ERICH: Law. Third term. *(He aims.)* Industrial
   law.
   (He fires.)
VALERIE: Industrial law. Isn't that rather boring?
ERICH *(loading)*: Good prospects. One day I should be a
   corporation lawyer. *(He aims.)* In industry.
   (He fires.)
VALERIE: And what do you think of our Vienna?
ERICH: Magnificently baroque.
VALERIE: And what about the sweet little Viennese girls?
ERICH: To be quite frank, I don't get on very well with

young girls. Actually, I've already been engaged, but
I was bitterly disillusioned, because Käthe was just
too young to be able to bring the right kind of understanding to bear on the problems of my ego. With
young girls you're wasting your feelings at the wrong
address. I'd much rather someone more mature, someone who can give as well as take.

(He fires.)

VALERIE: Where are you living?

ERICH: I'm thinking of moving.

VALERIE: I might have a furnished room.

ERICH: Cheap?

VALERIE: Dirt cheap.

ERICH: That'd be splendid.

(He fires.)

VALERIE: Well, Mr. Corporation Lawyer ... go on, let me
have a go.

ERICH: My pleasure.

VALERIE: No, my pleasure. *(She takes the gun from him.)*
Did you fight in the war?

ERICH: Alas, no. I was born in 1911.

VALERIE: 1911.

(She takes a long time aiming.)

ERICH *(giving the commands)*: Attention! Take aim! Fire!
*(VALERIE doesn't fire. She lowers the gun slowly and
looks at him intently.)*
What's the matter?

VALERIE: Ow! *(Suddenly, she doubles up, whimpering.)*
I get these shooting pains. My poor kidneys ...
(Silence.)

ERICH: Is there anything I can do?

VALERIE: No, thanks. I'm all right now. It quite often
happens when I get excited. I always suffer for it.

I don't know what I'm aiming at any more ...

ERICH *(confused)*: What do you mean, what you're aiming at?

VALERIE: That's because it's getting dark. *(She embraces him, he lets it happen. They kiss.)* It's always worth trying to get what you're aiming at. If you've nothing to aim for, you're not human any more. You. Mr. Nineteen hundred and eleven.

IV

BY THE BEAUTIFUL BLUE DANUBE

By now, the sun has gone down, it's already getting dark, and in the distance auntie's portable gramophone is play-ing Johann Strauss's waltz Frühlingsstimmen.

ALFRED, in a bathrobe and straw hat, is staring dreamily across at the opposite bank. MARIANNE climbs out of the beautiful blue Danube and sees ALFRED. Silence. ALFRED lifts his hat.

ALFRED: I knew you'd come ashore here.

MARIANNE: How did you know?

ALFRED: I just knew.

(Silence.)

MARIANNE: The Danube's so soft, it's like velvet.

ALFRED: Like velvet.

MARIANNE: I'd like to be somewhere else, far away, today. Tonight you could sleep out in the open.

ALFRED: Easily.

MARIANNE: Oh, we're just slaves of civilisation. What's become of our real natures?

ALFRED: We've turned our real natures into a strait-jacket. Nobody's allowed to do what they want to do.

41

MARIANNE: And nobody wants to do what they're allowed to do.
> *(Silence.)*

ALFRED: And nobody's allowed to do what they're able to do.

MARIANNE: And nobody's able to do what they ought to do.
> *(ALFRED embraces her dramatically and she makes no*
> *move to resist him. A long kiss.)*

MARIANNE *(gets her breath)*: I knew it, I knew it ...

ALFRED: So did I.

MARIANNE: Do you love me the way you ought to ...?

ALFRED: I feel as if I do. Let's sit down.
> *(They sit down. Silence.)*

MARIANNE: I'm so glad you're not stupid. I mean,
I'm surrounded by nothing but stupid people. Even
Papa's not what you'd call a bright spark. And
sometimes I think he just wants to use me to revenge
himself on my poor dear mother. She was very stubborn,
you see.

ALFRED: You think too much.

MARIANNE: I'm feeling good now. I feel like singing. I
always want to sing when I'm sad. *(She starts humming
and then stops again.)* Why aren't you saying anything?
> *(Silence.)*

ALFRED: Do you love me?

MARIANNE: Very much.

ALFRED: The way you ought to? I mean, sensibly?

MARIANNE: Sensibly?

ALFRED: I mean, I wouldn't like you to do anything rash.
I couldn't take the responsibility.

MARIANNE: Don't brood, there's no need to brood, look at
the stars. They'll still be up there in the sky when
we're lying down here in the earth.

ALFRED: I'm going to be cremated.

MARIANNE: So am I. You're ... oh, you're ... you ...

(Silence.)

MARIANNE: You've ... you've struck me like lightning and split me in two. But now I know. I know for certain.

ALFRED: What?

MARIANNE: That I'm not going to marry him.

ALFRED: Marianne!

MARIANNE: What's the matter?

(Silence.)

ALFRED: I haven't any money.

MARIANNE: What's that got to do with it?

ALFRED: It's my absolute basic duty. I've never destroyed someone's engagement, never in my life. On principle. Falling in love, yes, but making people split up because of it, no, I just don't have the moral right. I feel that way on principle.

(Silence.)

MARIANNE: I was right about you, you are a sensitive man. Now I feel doubly yours. I just don't suit Oskar and that's all there is to it.

(Meanwhile, it's got dark and fireworks are being set off nearby.)

ALFRED: Rockets. To celebrate your engagement.

MARIANNE: To celebrate our engagement.

ALFRED: And Bengal lights.

MARIANNE: Blue, green, yellow, red ...

ALFRED: They'll be out looking for you.

MARIANNE: I don't care if they find us. Stay with me, you've been sent down from Heaven, you're my guardian angel ...

(Bengal lights - blue, green, yellow, red - go up and light up ALFRED and MARIANNE and the ZAUBERKÖNIG, who is standing in front of them with his hand on his heart. MARIANNE stifles a cry. Silence.

43

ALFRED goes up to the ZAUBERKÖNIG.)

ALFRED: Herr Zauberkönig ...

ZAUBERKÖNIG *(interrupting him)*: Be quiet! You don't need
    to explain, I've heard everything. This is an absolute
    scandal! On the day of the engagement! Lying around
    naked! That's very nice, isn't it? Marianne! Get
    dressed! Suppose Oskar comes. Jesus, Mary and
    Joseph preserve us!

ALFRED: Naturally I shall take the consequences, if
    necessary.

ZAUBERKÖNIG: There'll be no consequences. All you have to
    do, you ... sir, is run for it. I will not allow this
    engagement to be ruined, for moral reasons or any other
    reasons. So you'd better make sure no-one finds out
    about this, you good-for-nothing. Promise me on your
    word of honour!

ALFRED: I promise.

MARIANNE: No!

ZAUBERKÖNIG *(through his teeth)*: Will you not shout! Are
    you ready? Hurry up and get dressed, come on, at the
    double. You slut!
    *(OSKAR appears and takes in the situation at a
    glance.)*

OSKAR: Marianne! Marianne!

ZAUBERKÖNIG: Disaster!
    (Silence.)

ALFRED: Your fiancée's been swimming, she's only just this
    minute come out.

MARIANNE: Don't lie! Just don't tell lies! I haven't
    been swimming, I've no intention of going swimming.
    I'm not going to let myself be tyrannised by you.
    The slave is snapping her chains ... there! *(She
    throws her engagement ring in OSKAR's face.)* I'm

44

not going to let my life be ruined, it's my life! At
the last minute God has sent me this man. So I'm
not, I'm not going to marry you, I'm not going to
marry you, I'm not going to marry you! As far as I'm
concerned, the toyshop can sink into the ground, and
the sooner the better!

ZAUBERKÖNIG: My only child! I'll remember that!

*(Silence. During MARIANNE's outburst, the other
picnickers have appeared and are listening with
malicious interest. OSKAR steps up to MARIANNE.)*

OSKAR: Marianne, I hope you'll never have to go through
what's happening to me now. I'm going to go on loving
you, you won't escape from me. And thank you for
everything.

(He exits. Silence.)

ZAUBERKÖNIG *(to ALFRED)*: Who do you think you are?

ALFRED: Me?

VALERIE: Nothing. He's a nothing.

ZAUBERKÖNIG: A nothing. On top of everything else. Well,
I don't have a daughter any more.

*(He exits with the picnickers. ALFRED and MARIANNE
are alone. The moon is shining.)*

ALFRED: I'm sorry. Forgive me ...

(MARIANNE gives him her hand.)

... for not having wanted you just now, I mean. I
feel responsible, that's what was responsible for it.
I'm not worthy of your love, I can't offer you any
sort of a life, I'm not really a man at all ...

MARIANNE: Nothing's going to shake me now. Let me make you
into a man. You make me feel so big and important ...

ALFRED: And you give me a kind of uplift. On the spiritual
plane I feel really small compared to you.

MARIANNE: You bring me out of myself, I'm watching myself

go. See, I'm really far away from myself now. I'm
right back there, I can hardly see myself any more.
I want to have your child...

Act Two

Back in the quiet street in Vienna 8, in front of OSKAR's butcher's shop, the dolls' hospital and VALERIE's tobacconist's. The sun is shining as before, and upstairs the schoolgirl is still playing Johann Strauss's Tales From The Vienna Woods.

HAVLITSCHEK is standing in the doorway of the butcher's, devouring a sausage. EMMA, a girl who's ready for anything, is standing next to him, holding a shopping-bag and listening to the music.

EMMA: Herr Havlitschek ...
HAVLITSCHEK: What can I do you for?
EMMA: There's something nice about music, isn't there?
HAVLITSCHEK: I can think of something a good deal nicer, Fräulein Emma.

    (EMMA hums along quietly with the waltz.)

    But that needs some work from your end, eh, Fräulein Emma?
EMMA: I think you're a bit of a Casanova, Herr Havlitschek.
HAVLITSCHEK: You can call me Ladislaus if you like.

    (Pause.)

EMMA: I had a dream about your Herr Oskar last night.
HAVLITSCHEK: Can't you find nothing more exciting to dream about than that?

EMMA: He's got them great big sad eyes, Herr Oskar. It
really upsets you when he looks at you.

HAVLITSCHEK: That's what love does for you.

EMMA: How do you mean?

HAVLITSCHEK: What I mean is, he fell in love with this bit
of shoddy goods, and she just up and left him, must
be a year ago now, and went off with some other bit
of shoddy goods.

EMMA: And he still loves her? I think that's nice.

HAVLITSCHEK: I think it's bloody ridiculous.

EMMA: A grand passion, there's something romantic about
it ...

HAVLITSCHEK: There's something sick about it, ask me.
Just look at the way he looks, he's torturing himself.
He won't look twice at another woman, and all the
while he's worth a packet and he's a well set-up
bloke, he could marry any one of a dozen women, and
not one of them rubbish, any time he felt like it. But
no, he's stuck on that little bitch on heat. Christ
knows what he does for it.

EMMA: How do you mean, Herr Havlitschek?

HAVLITSCHEK: Well, I mean, I can't think how he sweats
it off.

EMMA: Oo, you are disgusting.

(Pause.)

HAVLITSCHEK: I'm off tomorrow, Fräulein Emma, and I shall
be at the 68 bus terminus.

EMMA: I can't manage before three.

HAVLITSCHEK: No problem.

(Pause.)

EMMA: Half past three, then. And don't forget what you
promised, you said you wouldn't be naughty,
Ladislaus ...

48

(She exits.   HAVLITSCHEK watches her go and spits out the sausage-skin.)

HAVLITSCHEK: Stupid bitch, stupid ...

(OSKAR steps out of the butcher's.)

OSKAR: Don't forget, will you? We have to stick the pig today. You do it, I don't really fancy it today.

(Pause.)

HAVLITSCHEK: May I have a word with you, Herr Oskar, you don't mind if I say what I think, do you?

OSKAR: Is it about the pig?

HAVLITSCHEK: More of a sow than a pig, really. Herr Oskar, don't take it to heart like this, please, all this with your old fiancée, look, women, they're common as dirt. Anyone can get a woman, cripples, anyone, even if they're falling apart with the pox. And where it counts they're all the same, women, believe me, I'm being honest with you. They got no soul, women, it's just surface meat. And you shouldn't spoil a woman either, that's a big mistake, all they need's a good punch in the mouth every now and then, something like that.

(Pause.)

OSKAR: Woman is an enigma, Havlitschek. Like the Sphinx. I've taken samples of Marianne's handwriting round to various graphologists. The first one said, ah, this is the handwriting of a vampire, the second one said she'd make a really good friend, and the third one said she's the ideal housewife personified. An angel.

A FURNISHED ROOM IN VIENNA 18

Extremely cheap. About seven o'clock in the morning.
ALFRED is still in bed, smoking a cigarette. MARIANNE
is cleaning her teeth. An old pram in the corner and
nappies hanging on the line. Grey day, dim light.

MARIANNE *(gargling)*: You once said I was an angel. I
    told you then I wasn't an angel, I was just an
    ordinary girl with no ambitions. But you're so cold
    and calculating.
ALFRED: I'm not calculating, you know I'm not.
MARIANNE: Yes, you are. *(She fixes her hair.)* I must
    get a haircut.
ALFRED: So must I.
    (Silence.)
ALFRED: Marianne. What you getting up so early for?
MARIANNE: Because I can't sleep.
    (Silence.)
ALFRED: Are you unhappy?
MARIANNE: Aren't you?
    (They stare at each other.)
ALFRED: Who was it ruined the racing for me? I haven't
    spoken to a bookmaker, let alone a tipster, for a
    whole year. So I'm buggered here, aren't I?
    A new season, new favourites, two-year-olds,
    three-year-olds ... there's a new generation I have no
    contact with at all. And why don't I? Because I have
    to flog my guts out trying to sell a skin cream
    nobody buys because it's muck.
MARIANNE: People just don't have any money.
ALFRED: That's right, make excuses for people.

MARIANNE: You can't help it, I'm not blaming you.

ALFRED: I should bloody well hope not!

MARIANNE: Well, it's hardly my fault, the economic crisis.

ALFRED: Oh, you're so selfish. Who was it came up with the insane idea I should spend my life rushing round trying to sell cosmetics? It was you. *(He gets out of bed.)* Where are my suspenders?

(MARIANNE points to a chair.)

MARIANNE: There.

ALFRED: No.

MARIANNE: Then they're on the bedside cabinet.

ALFRED: No.

MARIANNE: Then I don't know where they are.

ALFRED: It's your job to know where they are.

MARIANNE: You're just like Papa.

ALFRED: Will you stop comparing me with that old moron!

MARIANNE: Don't shout! If you wake the baby, it'll finish me, all that crying.

(Silence.)

ALFRED: And that's another thing, something's got to be done about the baby. We can't just sit here, all three of us, rotting in this hole. The baby's going to have to go.

MARIANNE: The baby's staying right here.

ALFRED: The baby's got to go.

MARIANNE: No. Never.

(Silence.)

ALFRED: Where are my suspenders?

(MARIANNE looks at him, wide-eyed.)

MARIANNE: Do you know what day it is today?

ALFRED: No.

MARIANNE: It's the twelfth.

(Silence.)

ALFRED: So what?

MARIANNE: It's our anniversary. A year ago today I saw
     you for the first time. In the window.

ALFRED: I don't know why you always have to talk in
     hieroglyphics. We're not Egyptians, you know. What
     window?

MARIANNE: I was just arranging the skeleton and you knocked
     on the window. And then I let the blind down, because
     I suddenly got scared.

ALFRED: That's right.

MARIANNE: I was very lonely ...

     (She starts weeping, softly.)

ALFRED: Look, don't start snivelling again ... Listen,
     Marianne, I understand your maternal possessiveness
     a hundred per cent, but it's in the baby's interest to
     get him out of this damp hole. It's so grey and
     gloomy here, and at my mother's out in the Wachau,
     it's sunny.

MARIANNE: Well ...

ALFRED: That's settled, then!

     (Silence.)

MARIANNE: Fate weaves the pattern of our lives ...
     (She suddenly stares at ALFRED.) What did you
     say?

ALFRED: What?

MARIANNE: You said, stupid cow.

ALFRED: What are you talking about?

MARIANNE: Don't deny it!

     (ALFRED is cleaning his teeth and gargling.)
     You ought not to insult me all the time.
     *(Silence. ALFRED is putting shaving cream on his
     face.)*

52

ALFRED: My dear child, if there's one thing I hate from
    the bottom of my heart, it's stupidity. And sometimes
    you are quite outstandingly stupid. I can't understand
    why you're so stupid. It's not necessary, you know, to
    be so stupid.
    (Silence.)
MARIANNE: You once said I gave you a kind of uplift ...
    on the spiritual plane ...
ALFRED: I never said that. I can't possibly have said
    that. And if I did, I was wrong.
MARIANNE: Alfred!
ALFRED: Don't shout! Remember the baby.
MARIANNE: I'm so frightened, Alfred ...
ALFRED: You're imagining things.
MARIANNE: I mean, if you've really forgotten everything
    already ...
ALFRED: Crap!

III

A SMALL CAFÉ IN VIENNA 2

*FERDINAND VON HIERLINGER is playing billiards against
himself. ALFRED enters.*

HIERLINGER: Hello, Alfred! Good to see you again.
    Bit of a long face, why's that?
ALFRED: I've got a lot of worries.
HIERLINGER: Worrying never did anyone any good.
    Come on, give us a game, take your mind off it. *(He
    hands him a cue.)* First one to fifty, you break.
ALFRED: Bon. *(He miscues.)* Pathetic.
HIERLINGER *(taking his shot)*: Is it true you're working

53

in the bank again?

ALFRED: Nothing else going.

HIERLINGER: Cherchez la femme! When you fall in love,
    your brains are in your arse.

ALFRED: My dear Ferdinand, it's not a question of brains
    or keeping a cool head, it's to do with quite another
    organ. *(He puts his hand on his heart.)* There's a
    story by Hans Christian Andersen about the wicked
    boy shooting an arrow right into some poor old poet's
    heart. Cupid, Ferdinand, the god Cupid.

HIERLINGER *(concentrating on his break)*: Should have
    pulled it out again.

ALFRED: Thing is, I'm very soft-hearted, and she appealed
    to my youthful idealism. To start with, there was a
    certain amount of standard passion involved, and then,
    when the initial attraction had worn off, I started
    to feel sorry for her. I mean, she's the type of girl
    the right man wouldn't mind mothering, although she
    can be a spiteful little bitch sometimes. My God, I
    think I'm infatuated with her.

HIERLINGER: Infatuation's something in your blood. It's
    something to do with blood-heat.

ALFRED: Is that true?

HIERLINGER: Course it is. You're on. Eleven.
    (ALFRED plays a shot.)
    Alfred. Do you know what really knocked me back?
    Having a baby in the middle of the depression ...

ALFRED: Well, God knows, I never wanted her to have a
    baby, the whole thing was her idea and it just sort of
    happened. I would have got rid of it straight away,
    no trouble at all, but she wouldn't have that, she
    was quite fanatical about it, and then I had to lean
    on her very heavily before I could persuade her to go

54

through with it ... and what a pantomime that turned
out to be! Worse than useless and it still cost a
fortune. My God. You can't expect anything but bad
luck and you just have to put up with it.
*(MARIANNE appears. ALFRED sees her and calls over
to her.)*
Sit over there, will you? I'm just finishing my
game.
*(MARIANNE sits at a table and leafs through fashion
magazines. Silence.)*

HIERLINGER: Is that your lady?

ALFRED: Yup.

(Silence.)

HIERLINGER: So that's your lady. Funny. My good friend
Alfred's been living with a girl like that for over
a year now and this is the first time I've clapped
eyes on her. I thought it was only supposed to be
the jealous Turks who kept their favourites locked
away from their best friends.

ALFRED: In this case it's the other way round. It's not
me, it's her who's cut me off from my best friends...

HIERLINGER *(interrupting him)*: By the way, what's her name?

ALFRED: Marianne. *(Silence.)* What do you think?

HIERLINGER: I pictured her different.

ALFRED: In what way?

HIERLINGER: Bit more buxom.

ALFRED: More buxom than that?

HIERLINGER: Don't know why. You can't help it, you get
these pictures in your mind.

(Silence.)

ALFRED: She is quite buxom. Buxomer than you'd think.

(Silence.)

HIERLINGER: Bloody hell, that was a monumentally stupid

55

thing to do, wasn't it, breaking up with the mad tobac-
conist. You'd've been well stocked and fancy free.
ALFRED: No sense going on about the past. You'd be better
off helping me get out of this disastrous set-up as
painlessly as possible for all concerned.
HIERLINGER: Easier said than done. I don't suppose it's a
bed of roses, I mean financially speaking.
ALFRED: It's a bed of thorns, Ferdinand. A bed of thorns
and stinging nettles, like old Job had.
HIERLINGER: Where's the baby?
ALFRED: At my mother's. Out in the Wachau. At last!
HIERLINGER: Well, that's a help. Now the next thing I
would try and do is fix your Marianne up with something that'll make her financially independent, find
some way of sticking her into some profession. It's
well known that when a woman has a profession, it
gradually undermines any kind of relationship, even
marriage. That's the Church's main argument, that's
why they're fighting against women getting jobs, because the effect is to break up the family. They're
not idiots, you know, the cardinals, they're the
crème de la crème, they're the cleverest people we've
got.
ALFRED: Yes, I know. But Marianne's not trained for any
profession. The only thing she's interested in is
eurhythmics.
HIERLINGER: Big demand for eurhythmics.
ALFRED: Is that true?
HIERLINGER: Course it is.
ALFRED: I don't think I'm capable of thinking any more.
HIERLINGER: After all, eurhythmics is really only an off-
shoot of dancing, and that could be the light at the end
of the tunnel. See, I have a friend in the dancing world,

a baroness with international connections, who puts
together ballets and that kind of thing for very
classy establishments, might well be a possibility
there. Apart from anything else, the baroness owes
me a favour.

ALFRED: Well, I'd be eternally grateful to you ...

HIERLINGER: I'm your friend, that's good enough for me.
Tell you what, if I go now, I can catch the baroness
at her bridge party. So, I'll see you, Alfred. Do
me a favour, settle up for the coffee, will you? Chin
up, you'll be hearing from me, everything'll be all right.
*(He exits. ALFRED, holding his cue, slowly approaches
MARIANNE and sits at her table.)*

MARIANNE: Who won?

ALFRED: I lost. That's because I'm lucky in love. *(He
smiles, then suddenly stares at her neck.)* What's
that?

MARIANNE: This? It's a lucky charm.

ALFRED: What kind of a lucky charm?

MARIANNE: It's St. Anthony.

ALFRED: St. Anthony? How long have you had that?
(Silence.)

MARIANNE: Since I was little, whenever I lost anything,
I just had to say, St. Anthony, help me, and I'd
find it again.
(Silence.)

ALFRED: Is that supposed to be symbolic?

MARIANNE: It was just ...
(Silence.)

ALFRED: Personally I don't believe in a life after death,
although of course I believe in a Higher Being, that's
obvious, otherwise we wouldn't be here. Anyway,
St. Anthony, you listen to this, I've got something to
tell you, might turn out to be important ...

57

IV

AT HOME WITH THE BARONESS WITH INTERNATIONAL CONNECTIONS

*HELENE, the BARONESS's blind sister, is sitting in the
drawing-room at the spinet, improvising. FERDINAND
VON HIERLINGER enters with MARIANNE, shown in by the
SERVANT. HELENE breaks off her improvisation.*

HELENE: Anna! Who's that?

SERVANT: It's Herr von Hierlinger and a young lady.

    (He exits.)

HIERLINGER: Enchanté, countess.

    (HELENE stands up and gropes her way towards him.)

HELENE: Oh, good afternoon, Herr von Hierlinger. How very
    nice to see you again ...

HIERLINGER: Pleasure's all mine, countess. Is the
    baroness in?

HELENE: Yes, my sister's at home, but at the moment she's
    busy with the plumber. I put something I shouldn't have
    down the drain the other day and everything's blocked
    up. Who's that you've brought with you, Herr von Hierlinger?

HIERLINGER: A young lady with a great interest in
    eurhythmics. The baroness knows about her already.
    May I introduce ...

HELENE *(interrupting him)*: Very pleased to meet you!
    I'm afraid I can't see you, but you have a very
    sympathetic hand. Leave me your hand a minute,
    little lady of the hand ...

HIERLINGER: Countess Helene has an amazing talent for
    palm-reading.

    (Silence.)

MARIANNE: What sort of hand have I got?

58

(HELENE is still holding her tightly by the hand.)

HELENE: It's not as simple as that, my dear, when you're
blind you have to use your sense of touch to find your
way around. You have not much experience behind you,
much more to come ...

MARIANNE: What sort of thing?

*(The BARONESS enters unnoticed, wearing a cosmetic
face-mask, and listens.)*

HELENE: I would almost go so far as to say, this is the hand
of a sensualist. You have a child as well, don't you?

MARIANNE: Yes.

HIERLINGER: Fantastic! Fantastic!

HELENE: Boy or girl?

MARIANNE: Boy.

(Silence.)

HELENE: Yes, your son's going to give you a lot of joy.
He's going to turn out all right.

MARIANNE *(smiling)*: Really?

BARONESS: Helene! What is all this nonsense? You're not a
gypsy! You'd be better off trying not to block up the
lavatory again, my God, the filth out there! You
reading palms! That's a paradox, if ever I heard
one!

(She takes off her face-mask.)

HELENE: Oh, I have my premonitions.

BARONESS: Well, be so good as to confine your premonitions to the lavatory. It's costing me five schillings
again to get all that filth cleaned up! Anyone would
think I was living off you, not you off me!

(Silence.)

Well, Hierlinger dear, I expect this is the young lady
you telephoned me about the day before yesterday.

HIERLINGER: That's right. *(Quietly.)* And don't forget

one good turn deserves another.

(*The BARONESS threatens him playfully, shaking her
forefinger at him.*)

BARONESS: Blackmail?

HIERLINGER: Don't point, it's rude to point.

BARONESS: I know you're a man of honour. (*She leaves
him looking poisonously at her, crosses to MARIANNE
and walks round her, studying her from every angle.*)
Hm. Well, Fräulein, you say you have a great interest
in eurhythmics?

MARIANNE: Yes.

BARONESS: And you'd like to find some practical use for
your interest?

MARIANNE: Yes.

BARONESS: Can you sing?

MARIANNE: Sing?

BARONESS: I operate on the principle that there's no such
thing as can't. You can do anything if you set your
mind to it! The dance groups I put together are
international attractions at first-class night-clubs.
So you can't sing?

MARIANNE: I'm afraid ...

BARONESS: Didn't you learn to sing at school?

MARIANNE: Oh, yes.

BARONESS: Well, then! I just want to hear your voice.
Surely you know a nice Viennese song, you're Viennese,
aren't you? Some nice folksong ...

MARIANNE: What about the Song of the Wachau?

BARONESS: That'll do fine. Off you go. The Song of the Wachau.
(*MARIANNE sings, HELENE at the spinet.*)

MARIANNE: Es kam einst gezogen ein Bursch ganz allein
        Und wanderte froh in den Abend hinein.
        Da flog ein Lächeln ihm zu und ein Blick.

60

Er dachte noch lange daran zurück.

Ein rosiges Antlitz, ein goldener Schopf,

Zwei leuchtende Augen, ein Mädchenkopf.

Das Mädel, das ging ihm nicht mehr aus dem Sinn,

Und oft sang er vor sich hin:

Da draussen in der Wachau

Die Donau fliesst so blau,

Steht einsam ein Winzerhaus,

Da schaut ein Mädel heraus.

Hat Lippen rot wie Blut,

Und küssen kanns so gut,

Die Augen sind veilchenblau

Vom Mädel in der Wachau.

V

OUT IN THE WACHAU

*Here too the sun is shining as before, only now an old
pram stands in front of the cottage.*

MOTHER *(to ALFRED)*: He looks just like you, little Leopold.
    And he doesn't cry much either. You were very good
    too, when you were a baby.

ALFRED: I'm just glad I haven't got him in Vienna. He'll
    do much better out here in the good air, than he
    would have done living in our barracks.

MOTHER: Has Marianne started at the ballet yet?

ALFRED: No, not till next Saturday.

    (Silence.)

MOTHER *(anxiously)*: You used to say if you had a child
    you'd get married. Do you still feel the same way?

ALFRED: You used to say I could make a good match.

    (Silence.)

MOTHER: Well, naturally this particular relationship is rather unfortunate.

ALFRED: May I have a word with Granny now?

MOTHER: I'll go and tell her. I have to go back to the cellar now anyway.

    (She exits into the cottage. ALFRED, alone, bends over the pram and contemplates his child. His GRANDMOTHER emerges from the cottage.)

GRANDMOTHER: What can I do for you, young man?

ALFRED: Have you thought about it?

GRANDMOTHER: I don't have any money. As long as you're living with that person, I don't have any money. You live there with your concubine like dogs in a kennel, you bring bastards into the world and palm them off on other people, and then you have the face to come and ask your old granny for more money. Not a penny! Not one penny!

ALFRED: That your last word?

GRANDMOTHER: Dogs in a kennel, dogs in a kennel!

ALFRED: Old witch.

    (Silence.)

GRANDMOTHER: What did you say?

    (ALFRED says nothing.)

    You wouldn't dare say that again.

ALFRED: I would.

GRANDMOTHER: Go on, then.

ALFRED: Witch. Old witch.

    (His GRANDMOTHER comes up to him slowly and pinches his arm. He smiles.)

    What's that supposed to be?

GRANDMOTHER *(pinching him)*: You just wait, you'll feel it

in a minute. There. There.

(ALFRED, who is now beginning to feel something, shakes her off.)

ALFRED: I don't mind human beings trying to hurt me, but not frogs.

GRANDMOTHER *(weeping with rage)*: Give me my money back, you great lout! I want my money, you hooligan, you thief!

(ALFRED laughs.)

(Shrieking) Stop laughing!

(She fetches him a blow with her walking-stick.)

ALFRED: Ow!

GRANDMOTHER *(grinning with satisfaction)*: You felt that? You felt that all right, did you?

ALFRED: You witch. You old witch.

(His GRANDMOTHER lifts her stick triumphantly.)

Don't you dare!

GRANDMOTHER: I'll do what I like, you stupid boy. I could still knock you down, you know, I could still knock anyone down. Tut, you've got another button hanging off there. How you can live with such a slovenly bitch, I ...

ALFRED *(interrupting her)*: She's certainly not slovenly!

(Silence.)

GRANDMOTHER: Her mouth is far too big.

ALFRED: That's a matter of taste.

GRANDMOTHER: Just a minute, I'll sew your button on for you. *(She does so.)* What d'you need a woman for, when you've got your old granny to sew your buttons on for you? Not that you're worth looking after, taking up with a beggar-woman and having a child by her, a child!

ALFRED: These things can happen.

GRANDMOTHER: You're so thoughtless, so thoughtless!

63

ALFRED: You know I pulled out all the stops, there was
    just nothing I could do about it.
    (Silence.)
GRANDMOTHER: Poor unfortunate devil, you are, Alfred.
ALFRED: Why?
GRANDMOTHER: Because you're always falling into the clutches
    of women like that ...
    (Silence.)
    Listen, Alfred. If you leave your precious Marianne,
    I'll lend you some money ...
    (Silence.)
ALFRED: What?
GRANDMOTHER: You heard me.
    (Silence.)
ALFRED: How much?
GRANDMOTHER: You're still young and handsome ...
    (ALFRED points at the pram.)
ALFRED: What about that?
GRANDMOTHER: Don't worry about that. Just go away
    somewhere.
    (Silence.)
ALFRED: Where?
GRANDMOTHER: France. Everything's still going well over
    there, I read it in the paper. If I were young, I'd
    be off to France first thing ...

    VI

    AND BACK IN THE QUIET STREET IN VIENNA 8

*It's already late afternoon and the schoolgirl on the
second floor is playing Johann Strauss's waltz Frühlingsstimmen. OSKAR stands in the doorway of his shop, cleaning
his fingernails with a penknife. The CAPTAIN enters, left,*

and nods to OSKAR. OSKAR bows.

CAPTAIN: Well, I really must say, that blood-sausage yes-
    terday. My compliments. First class.
OSKAR: Tender, wasn't it?
CAPTAIN: A poem.
    *(He approaches the tobacconist's. VALERIE appears
    in the doorway of the tobacconist's. The CAPTAIN
    greets her. VALERIE responds.)*
    May I have a look at the lottery results?
    *(VALERIE gets them from the rack by the door and hands
    them to him.)*
    Enchanté.
    *(He buries himself in the list of results and the
    waltz ends. The ZAUBERKÖNIG accompanies the LADY out
    of the dolls' hospital.)*
LADY: I bought some tin soldiers here once before, last
    year ... but then I was served by a very polite girl.
ZAUBERKÖNIG *(surly)*: Could be.
LADY: Was that your daughter?
ZAUBERKÖNIG: I have no daughter. I never had a daughter!
LADY: Pity. So, you won't order a box of tin soldiers
    for me?
ZAUBERKÖNIG: I explained it to you inside, ordering things
    is much too much paperwork, just for one box. Why
    don't you buy the little chappie something along the
    same lines? Like a nice trumpet perhaps?
LADY: No. Goodbye.
    (She leaves him there, annoyed, and exits.)
ZAUBERKÖNIG: Enchanté! Drop dead!
    (He exits into the dolls' hospital.)
VALERIE *(spitefully)*: And what have we won this time,
    captain?

(ERICH comes out of the tobacconist's and tries to leave quickly.)

VALERIE: Just a minute! What's that you've got?

ERICH: Five Memphis.

VALERIE: What again? He smokes like a grown-up.

(The CAPTAIN and OSKAR are listening.)

ERICH *(through his teeth)*: Look, if I don't smoke, I can't work. And if I don't work, I'll never get to be a barrister. And if I don't, there's hardly any chance I shall ever be in a position to be able to pay back my debts.

VALERIE: What debts?

ERICH: You know very well. I'm scrupulous about these things, Madame.

VALERIE: Scrupulous? Are you trying to upset me again?

ERICH: Upset you? It's a matter of honour. I pay my debts down to the last penny, even if it takes me a hundred years! We don't leave ourselves open to comment, you know, it's a matter of honour! And now I must get to the college ...

(He exits.)

VALERIE *(staring after him)*: Matter of honour. Pig ...

(The CAPTAIN and OSKAR grin to themselves.)

CAPTAIN *(spitefully getting his own back)*: And how are things otherwise, Frau Valerie?

(ERICH suddenly reappears.)

ERICH *(to the CAPTAIN)*: Did I see you smirking just now? You, sir!

VALERIE *(nervously)*: Do you gentlemen know each other?

CAPTAIN: By sight.

ERICH: You're an Austrian. All mouth and no guts.

VALERIE: Erich!

CAPTAIN: What did he say?

66

ERICH: I said the Austrians were totally spineless in the
    war, and if it hadn't been for us Prussians ...
CAPTAIN *(finishing his sentence)*: ...there'd never have
    been a war at all!
ERICH: What about Sarajevo? What about Bosnia-
    Herzegovina?
CAPTAIN: What do you know about the world war, you whipper-
    snapper? What you were taught in school, that's all.
ERICH: Well, that's better than teaching old Jewesses to
    play bridge!
VALERIE: Erich!
CAPTAIN: Yes, and it's better than leeching off old
    tobacconists!
VALERIE: Captain!
CAPTAIN: I apologise. That was a faux pas. A lapsus
    linguae. *(He kisses her hand.)* It was deplorable,
    quite deplorable. But this greenhorn has never earned
    himself a penny in his whole life.
ERICH: Very well, sir!
VALERIE: No, not a duel, for God's sake!
ERICH: I assume you'd be prepared to give satisfaction.
CAPTAIN: You want to take me to court?
VALERIE: Jesus, Mary and Joseph!
ERICH: I do not allow myself to be insulted!
CAPTAIN: No-one's going to insult me and get away with it!
    Certainly not you!
VALERIE: Please, stop it, this is a scandal ...
    (She exits, sobbing, into the tobacconist's.)
CAPTAIN: I refuse to allow these things to be said about
    me by this Prussian. Where were your Hohenzollerns
    then, when our Habsburgs were already Holy Roman
    Emperors, tell me that? Still in the trees!
ERICH: That is the last straw.

CAPTAIN *(calling after him)*: Here's twenty groschen, get
     yourself a haircut, you great cockatoo! *(He
     turns and starts to exit left, then stops again in
     front of the butcher's. To OSKAR.)* By the way, I
     know what I meant to ask you: are you slaughtering
     the pig today?

OSKAR: I'm about to, captain.

CAPTAIN: Save me a nice bit of kidney, will you?

OSKAR: Be glad to, captain.

CAPTAIN: Enchanté.

     *(He exits, left, and upstairs the schoolgirl starts
     playing again, this time the waltz Über den Wellen.
     ALFRED strolls on, left. OSKAR is about to go back
     into the butcher's, but catches sight of ALFRED, who
     doesn't notice him, and watches him secretly. ALFRED
     stops in front of the dolls' hospital, reminiscing.
     Then he moves on to the open door of the tobacconist's
     and stands looking in. Pause. ALFRED nods.
     Pause. After a time, VALERIE appears in the doorway,
     and the waltz breaks off, again in mid-phrase.
     Silence.)*

ALFRED: Could I have five Memphis?

VALERIE: No.

     (Silence.)

ALFRED: This is a tobacconist's, isn't it?

VALERIE: No.

     (Silence.)

ALFRED: I just happened to be passing, by chance ...

VALERIE: Oh, yes?

ALFRED: Yes.

     (Silence.)

VALERIE: And how is the young sir?

ALFRED: So-so, you know.

VALERIE: And your young lady?

ALFRED: So-so.

VALERIE: Oh, yes?

(Silence.)

ALFRED: And you're all right, I hope?

VALERIE: I have everything I need.

ALFRED: Everything?

VALERIE: Everything. He's a law-student.

ALFRED: They'll take anything for lawyers nowadays.

VALERIE: What?

ALFRED: Congratulations.

(Silence.)

VALERIE: Where is poor Marianne?

ALFRED: I may well be losing sight of her ...

(Silence.)

VALERIE: You really are a champion bastard, aren't you, even your worst enemy would have to give you that.

ALFRED: Valerie, he that is without sin, let him cast the first stone at me.

VALERIE: Are you ill?

ALFRED: No. Just tired. And rushed off my feet. I'm not as young as I was.

VALERIE: Since when?

ALFRED: I'm going to France this evening. Nancy. I think I might be able to find something that'll suit me better, in the haulage business. I'd have to sink too far below my own standards if I stayed here.

VALERIE: What about the gee-gees?

ALFRED: Don't ask me! Anyway, where would I find the capital ...?

(Silence.)

VALERIE: If I get the time, I might feel sorry for you.

ALFRED: Would you like it, if things went badly for me?

VALERIE: I thought you hadn't a care in the world.

ALFRED: Would you like it, if that were true?

(Silence.)

I just happened to be passing through, by chance ...
felt a kind of melancholic nostalgia ... for my
old haunts ...

(He exits, and the waltz Über den Wellen starts up
once again.)

VALERIE (catching sight of OSKAR): Herr Oskar! Guess who
I've just been chatting to.

OSKAR: I saw.

VALERIE: Ah. Things are going badly for them.

OSKAR: I heard.

(Pause.)

VALERIE: He still has the pride of a Spaniard ...

OSKAR: Pride comes before a fall. Poor Marianne ...

VALERIE: I should think you could still marry her, now
she's on her own again ...

OSKAR: Yes, if it wasn't for the child ...

VALERIE: If anyone had done that to me ...

OSKAR: I still love her. Perhaps the child'll die ...

VALERIE: Herr Oskar!

OSKAR: Who knows? Though the mills of God grind slowly,
yet they grind extremely small. I shall never forget
my Marianne. I shall take all her sufferings on
myself, whom the Lord loveth, He chasteneth. He
scourgeth. He chastiseth. With red-hot irons and
molten lead ...

VALERIE (shouts at him): Stop it, please!

(OSKAR smiles. HAVLITSCHEK comes out of the butcher's.)

HAVLITSCHEK: Well, what's the story? Am I going to stick
the pig or am I not?

OSKAR: No, Havlitschek. I'm going to do it myself today,

70

I'll stick the pig ...

(Peal of bells.)

VII

IN ST. STEPHEN'S CATHEDRAL

*In front of St. Anthony's side-altar. MARIANNE is at
confession. The bells fall silent and all is peaceful.*

CONFESSOR: To recap, then: you've caused the most agonising
suffering and anxiety to your poor old father, who
loves you more than anything and only ever wanted the
best for you, you've been disobedient and ungrateful,
you've abandoned an admirable fiancé in order to bind
yourself to a degenerate, driven on by lust ... be
quiet! That much we've established. And now you've
been living with this wretched individual outside the
holy sacrament of marriage for over a year, and in this
appalling state of mortal sin, you've conceived and
given birth to a child. When was that?

MARIANNE: Eight weeks ago.

CONFESSOR: A child of shame and sin, and you've not even
had it baptised. Now tell me: do you think anything
good can come of all this? No, never! And as if that
wasn't enough, you didn't even shrink from wanting to
kill the child in your womb ...

MARIANNE: No, that was him! I only agreed to go through
with it because of him!

CONFESSOR: Only because of him?

MARIANNE: He didn't want to bring a child into the world,
because times are getting worse and worse and nobody
knows what's going to happen ... but I ... the fact I

71

tried to have an abortion, every time the baby looks
at me, I can't bear to think of it.
    (Silence.)
CONFESSOR: Did you keep it?
MARIANNE: No.
CONFESSOR: Where is it?
MARIANNE: With relatives. Out in the Wachau.
CONFESSOR: Godfearing people?
MARIANNE: I'm sure they are.
    (Silence.)
CONFESSOR: So you repent having wanted to kill it?
MARIANNE: Yes.
CONFESSOR: And living out of wedlock with that brute?
    (Silence.)
MARIANNE: I thought I'd found the man who would make my
    life complete ...
CONFESSOR: Do you repent?
    (Silence.)
MARIANNE: Yes.
CONFESSOR: And having conceived and given birth to a child
    in a state of mortal sin, do you repent that too?
    (Silence.)
MARIANNE: No. You can't ...
CONFESSOR: What's that?
MARIANNE: He is my child, after all ...
CONFESSOR: But you're ...
MARIANNE *(interrupting him)*: I'm not going to. No. I'd
    be frightened to think I could repent that. No,
    I'm happy I have him, very happy ...
    (Silence.)
CONFESSOR: If you're not able to repent, what is it you
    expect from the Lord?
MARIANNE: I thought perhaps He would have something to
72

tell me ...

CONFESSOR: You only come to Him when things are going
   badly?

MARIANNE: When things are going well, I think He's with
   me anyway ... but He can't want me to repent a thing
   like that ... that would be completely unnatural ...

CONFESSOR: Then go away! And until you can come to terms
   with yourself, don't appear before Our Lord again.

   (He makes the sign of the cross.)

MARIANNE: Then I'm sorry.

   (She gets up from the confessional, now melting into
   darkness, and the murmur of a litany is heard.
   Gradually the priest's voice can be distinguished
   from the voices of the congregation. MARIANNE
   listens: the litany ends with the Lord's Prayer.
   MARIANNE's lips move. Silence.)

   Amen.

   (Silence.)

   If there is a God ... what's to become of me, God?
   Dear God, I was born in Vienna 8 and I went to the
   local secondary school, I'm not a bad person ... are you
   listening? What's to become of me, God?

   (Silence.)

Act Three

AT THE TAVERN

Tavern music and falling blossom. Bibulous atmosphere. And,
in the thick of it, the ZAUBERKÖNIG, VALERIE and ERICH.
Everyone is singing:

ALL: Da draussen in der Wachau
        Die Donau fliesst so blau,
        Steht einsam ein Winzerhaus,
        Da schaut ein Mädel heraus.
        Hat Lippen rot wie Blut,
        Und küssen kanns so gut,
        Die Augen sind veilchenblau
        Vom Mädel in der Wachau.

        Es wird ein Wein sein,
        Und wir werden nimmer sein.
        Es wird schöne Madeln geben,
        Und wir werden nimmer leben ...

Now, for a moment, a deathly hush falls on the tavern ...
then everyone starts singing again, three times as
loud.

    Drum gehn wir gern nach Nussdorf naus,
    Da gibts a Hetz, a Gstanz,
    Da hörn wir ferme Tanz,

> Da lass ma fesche Jodler naus
>
> Und gengan in der Fruah
>
> Mitn Schwomma zhaus, mitn Schwomma zhaus!

Enthusiastic applause. Between the tables, people start dancing to the Radetzky March. *By now everyone is well away.*

ZAUBERKÖNIG: Bravo, bravissimo! I'm my old self today! Da capo, da capo! *(He grabs at a GIRL's breasts, as she dances by. Her BOYFRIEND slaps his hand.)*

BOYFRIEND: Hands off the tits!

GIRL: They're my tits.

ZAUBERKÖNIG: What's a tit between friends? Everyone has his troubles, but today I want to forget them all! I don't give a bugger for anything!

ERICH: Listen, everybody! I hereby propose a most lavish toast to the famous Viennese wine festival. Cheers! *(He spills his wine.)*

VALERIE: Don't get so worked up, boy! My God, it's spilt all over me.

ERICH: Accidents will happen. It's a matter of honour.

ZAUBERKÖNIG: Has he made you wet? You poor wee thing.

VALERIE: Soaked to the skin.

ZAUBERKÖNIG: To the skin, eh ···

VALERIE: Now, don't be cheeky.

ERICH: Attention!

(He clicks his heels and stands to attention.)

ZAUBERKÖNIG: What's the matter with him?

VALERIE: I'm used to it now. When he's plastered, he gives himself orders all the time.

ZAUBERKÖNIG: He's very good at it. Straight. Really straight. Bit of respect. We're on the way up again. *(He collapses under the table.)*

VALERIE: Jesus!

ZAUBERKÖNIG: This chair is broken. Waiter, another chair!
Hey, another chair! *(He sings along with the music.)*
'Ach, ich hab sie ja nur auf die Schulter geküsst ...
und schon hab ich den Patsch verspürt mit dem Fächer
ins Gesicht' ...

(A waiter brings a gigantic portion of salami.)

VALERIE: Salami, Erich! Salami!

ERICH: Company! Stand at ease!
*(He reaches into the bowl and starts guzzling at an
alarming rate.)*

ZAUBERKÖNIG: The way he shovels it in!

VALERIE: Bon appétit.

ZAUBERKÖNIG: Don't be so greedy!

VALERIE: One thing, he's not paying.

ZAUBERKÖNIG: And he can't even sing.

(Pause.)

VALERIE *(to ERICH)*: Why won't you sing?

ERICH *(with his mouth full)*: Because of my chronic sore
throat.

VALERIE: You smoke too much.

ERICH *(yelling at her)*: Don't start that again!
*(The CAPTAIN appears, wearing a little paper hat and
in high spirits.)*

CAPTAIN: Enchanté, my dear Frau Valerie. What a pleasant
surprise! Greetings, Herr Zauberkönig!

ZAUBERKÖNIG: Prost, captain, my dear captain, Prost!
*(He empties his glass, and lapses into a melancholy
stupor.)*

VALERIE: May I offer you some of my salami, captain?
*(ERICH stops in mid-chew and glares at the CAPTAIN
with hatred.)*

CAPTAIN: Too kind, enchanté. But no, I couldn't
possibly fit any more ... *(He sticks two thick slices*

76

into *his mouth.)* I've had two lots of dinner already
this evening, I've got a visitor ... I've been sitting
over there with him. He's a school friend of my brother
who went missing in Siberia: an American.

VALERIE: Ah, a Yank.

CAPTAIN: Born in Vienna, though. He's been over there in
the States for twenty years, and this is his first time
back in Europe. This morning when we drove through
the Hofburg, he had tears in his eyes. He's what they
call a self-made man. Does everything for himself.

VALERIE: Oo, you are dreadful!

CAPTAIN: Yes. And I'm showing him round his Vienna. This is
the second day. I'm afraid we'll never be sober again ...

VALERIE: Still waters run deep.

CAPTAIN: Yes, and not only in America.

ERICH *(aggressively)*: Oh, really?

> *(Pause.)*

VALERIE *(approaching ERICH)*: Behave yourself. And shut up,
or I'll clout you. If you're going to scoff all my
salami, I want a bit of consideration.

ERICH: That kind of remark is a tribute to your mean-
mindedness, Madame.

VALERIE: Stop it!

ERICH: Attention! Company ...

VALERIE: Halt!

ERICH: Company, by the left, quick march!

> *(He exits.)*

VALERIE *(calling after him)*: About turn! About turn!

> *(Deathly silence.)*

CAPTAIN: Who is that, anyway?

VALERIE *(tonelessly)*: He thinks he's a whole army. Soon
I'm going to leave him flat. I can see it coming.
(She points to the ZAUBERKÖNIG.) He's a distant

77

relation of that one.

(The music starts up again.)

CAPTAIN: Speaking of relations, tell me, Frau Valerie, do
you think it's right the way His Majesty Herr Zauberkönig has treated Fräulein Marianne? I can't understand it. If I was a grandfather ... I mean, anyway,
it's easy to make a mistake. But just to let things
go like that ...

VALERIE: Have you heard any more details, captain?

CAPTAIN: I once had a colonel's wife, that's to say, the
whole regiment had her ... what am I talking about?
I mean, she was the colonel's wife, and the colonel
had an illegitimate child by some girl from the music-
hall, but his wife took it in as if it were her own
flesh and blood, because, you see, she was barren.
Now, when you look at the way old Zauberkönig over
there has behaved, compared to that ... well, say no
more.

VALERIE: I don't understand, captain. What's the colonel's
wife got to do with Marianne?

CAPTAIN: People don't understand each other any more, Frau
Valerie. Quite often we don't understand ourselves.

VALERIE: Where is Marianne?

CAPTAIN *(smiling mysteriously)*: There will be an official
announcement about that, when the time is ripe.

(The AMERICAN appears: he is drunk.)

AMERICAN: My dear old friend ... what's this I see?
People? Friends? Introduce me, will you please?
Dear old friend ...

*(He embraces the CAPTAIN. The ZAUBERKÖNIG awakes from
his stupor.)*

ZAUBERKÖNIG: Who's that?

CAPTAIN: This is my friend from America.

AMERICAN: America! New York! Chicago! Sing Sing!
That's just on the outside: inside beats the old
honest to God real golden Viennese heart, eternal
Vienna ... and the Wachau ... and the castles by the
blue Danube. *(He hums along to the music.)* 'Donau
so blau, so blau, so blau' ...
(Everyone joins in, swaying in their seats.)
Ladies and gentlemen, there's been a lot of changes
lately, there's been storms and whirlwinds all over
the world, and earthquakes and tornadoes, and I had to
start right from the bottom, but I'm right at home
here, I know my way round here, I like it here, I want
to die here! With the Lord God of old Austria from
Mariazell! *(He sings)*:

> Mein Muatterl war a Wienerin,
>
> Drum hab ich Wien so gern.
>
> Sie wars, die mit dem Leben
>
> Mir die Liebe hat gegeben
>
> Zu meinem anzigen goldenen Wean!

(Everyone sings.)

ALL: Wien, Wien, nur du allein

> Sollst stets die Stadt meiner Träume sein,
>
> Dort, wo ich glücklich und selig bin,
>
> Ist Wien, ist Wien, mein Wien!

AMERICAN: Long live Vienna! Home! And the beautiful
Viennese women! And all the memories of home! And
long live the Viennese, all of us, every one, every
one!

ALL: Vienna!

(Everybody drinks.)

ZAUBERKÖNIG *(to VALERIE)*: And the beautiful Viennese
women, you magnificent creature. I should have
married you, with you I would've had a quite different

child.

VALERIE: I wish you wouldn't keep talking about Irene.
    I could never stand her!

AMERICAN: Who's Irene?

ZAUBERKÖNIG: Irene was my wife.

AMERICAN: Oh, pardon me.

ZAUBERKÖNIG: That's all right. Why shouldn't I complain
    about Irene? Just because she's dead? She ruined
    my whole life.

VALERIE: You're a devil.

ZAUBERKÖNIG *(sings)*:

> Mir ist mei Alte gstorbn,
>
> Drum ist mirs Herz so schwer.
>
> A so a gute Seel
>
> Krieg ich nöt mehr,
>
> Muss so viel wana,
>
> Das glaubt mir kana,
>
> Dass ich mich kränk,
>
> Wenn ich an mei Alte denk! Olé!

AMERICAN *(jumping up)*: Olé! Olé! Unless I'm very much
    mistaken, it's starting to rain. But we're not
    going to let the weather get in our way. Tonight
    we're going to take it easy, let the rain pitter-patter,
    but it really doesn't matter. *(He shakes a finger at
    the sky.)* You want to rain, do you? Rest of the even-
    ing's on me. You're all invited! Every one of you!
    (Enthusiastic response from everyone.)
    O.K. Off we go. Follow me!

VALERIE: Where to?

AMERICAN: Anywhere! Anywhere with a ceiling! So's we
    don't have to sit out in the open. The Moulin Bleu!
    (Loud applause.)

CAPTAIN: Wait! Not the Moulin Bleu, my friends. Let's

go to Maxim's!

(Again, for a moment, a deathly silence.)

ZAUBERKÖNIG: Why Maxim's?

CAPTAIN: Because there's a very special surprise waiting
for us there.

ZAUBERKÖNIG: What kind of a surprise?

CAPTAIN: Something spicy. Very spicy.

(Silence.)

ZAUBERKÖNIG: All right, Maxim's it is.

ALL: Maxim's.

(They march off with raised umbrellas, singing.)

ALL: Vindobona, du herrliche Stadt,

Die so reizende Anlagen hat,

Dir gehört stets nur unser Sinn.

Ja zu dir, da ziagts uns hin,

San ma a von dir oft fern,

Denkn ma do ans liebe Wean,

Denn du bleibst die Perle von Österreich,

Dir ist gar ka Stadt net gleich!

Die Mizzi und der Jean

Gehn Miteinander drahn,

Wir sind ja nicht aus Stroh,

Sind jung und lebensfroh,

Net immer Schokoladi,

Heut gehen wir zum 'Brady'

Oder zum 'Maxim'

Heut sind wir einmal schlimm!

Jetzt trink ma noch a Flascherl Wein,

Hollodero!

Es muss ja nöt das letzte sein

Hollodero!

Und ist das gar, gibts ka Geniern,

Hollodero!

So tun wir noch mal repetiern, aber noch mal repetiern!

(Gong. The stage is transformed into Maxim's. A bar and private booths. In the background a cabaret stage with a wide ramp. They all close their umbrellas and sit at the tables in the most expansive mood. The COMPÈRE steps out in front of the curtain.)

COMPÈRE: Honoured guests, ladies and gentlemen! Delightful ladies and even more delightful gentlemen!

VALERIE: Aha!

(Laughter.)

COMPÈRE: I bid you a most hearty welcome on behalf of the management! As Johann Wolfgang von Goethe, the prince of poets, says in his masterpiece, the immortal *Faust:* 'That which thy father bequeathed thee, earn it anew, if thou wouldst possess it.' In other words, ladies and gentlemen, we expect you all to join in the songs. That's the tradition of the house, ladies and gentlemen. And now, I want you to come with us down memory lane!

(The orchestra strikes up Johann Strauss's waltz Wiener Blut, the curtain goes up, and girls in Old Vienna costumes dance the waltz. Then the curtain falls. Tremendous enthusiasm from the audience and the orchestra plays the Hoch-und Deutschmeister March.)

ZAUBERKÖNIG *(to the CAPTAIN)*: What are you talking about? It's been established beyond the shadow of a doubt that we're descended from the animals.

CAPTAIN: It's open to debate.

ZAUBERKÖNIG: I suppose you believe in Adam and Eve.

CAPTAIN: Who knows?

82

AMERICAN *(to VALERIE)*: You bobcat!

ZAUBERKÖNIG: Bobcat! Or a leopard maybe.

VALERIE: Prost Zauberkönig!

ZAUBERKÖNIG: The captain is some fabulous beast, you have
   something of the kangaroo in you, and the Yank is a
   Japanese pug.

AMERICAN *(not laughing at all)*: You're a thousand laughs.

ZAUBERKÖNIG: And what about me?

VALERIE: You're a stag. An old stag. Prost, old stag!
   *(Roars of laughter. The table telephone rings.
   Silence.)*

ZAUBERKÖNIG *(answering)*: Hallo, yes? ... What? Who's
   that? Mousey?... Mousey, never heard of you. What?...
   Oh, I see, yes, that's right, that's right, I'm
   your uncle ... What do you want ? Oo, you devil, you
   little piggie ... Where? At the bar? In the
   green dress? ... What? You're still a virgin? You
   expect your old uncle to believe that? Well, I shall
   have to check, won't I?...
   *(He makes kissing sounds, hangs up and empties the
   glass of champagne the AMERICAN has ordered.)*

VALERIE: You shouldn't drink so much, Leopold.

ZAUBERKÖNIG: Take a running jump. *(He gets up.)* When
   you're as old as I am, alcohol's the only pleasure
   left. Where's the bar?

VALERIE: What bar?

ZAUBERKÖNIG: The bar, for Christ's sake!

CAPTAIN: I'll take you.

ZAUBERKÖNIG: I can find it myself, I don't need a guide
   dog! Come on then, show me!
   *(He lets the CAPTAIN lead him to the bar, where two
   girls are waiting for him. The one in the green dress
   gives him a warm welcome. The CAPTAIN stays by the*

bar as well.)

AMERICAN *(to VALERIE)*: What does he do?

VALERIE: Runs a toyshop.

AMERICAN: Oh.

VALERIE: Yes. Apart from that, he's a bit of a rarity, modest and respectable, a real representative of the old school. It's a dying breed.

AMERICAN: Pity.

VALERIE: Unfortunately, he's plastered today ...

AMERICAN: The way you said that. What charm! Back in the States, everything's so much more brutal.

VALERIE: How much do you weigh?

AMERICAN: Two hundred eighteen pounds.

VALERIE: My God!

AMERICAN: May I speak frankly?

VALERIE: Please do.

AMERICAN: I'm complicated.

VALERIE: How do you mean?

AMERICAN: I mean, inside, I'm dead. It's got so's I can only make out with prostitutes. That's because of the many disappointments in my past.

VALERIE: Who'd have thought it? Such a sensitive soul in such a huge body ...

AMERICAN: I was born under Saturn.

VALERIE: Yes, those old stars! We're stuck with them and there's nothing we can do about it.

(Gong. The COMPÈRE steps out in front of the curtain.)

COMPÈRE: And now, ladies and gentlemen, once again we have for you a wonderful act. I won't waste words describing it, judge for yourselves our sensational, highly artistic, and specially designed for us by the

most distinguished artists: our tableaux vivants.
And first, the Mermaids of the Danube! Maestro, if
you please!

*(The orchestra strikes up with The Blue Danube Waltz
and the house lights go out. Then the curtains
open to reveal three half-naked girls, legs encased
in tail-fins. One holds a lyre. They are
picturesquely grouped in front of a black curtain
lit by green spotlights. From the bar, the
ZAUBERKÖNIG's voice is heard.)*

ZAUBERKÖNIG: Naked women, I should think so too!

*(The curtains close to loud applause. Gong. The
COMPÈRE appears in front of the curtain again.)*

COMPÈRE: The second tableau: the Zeppelin!

(Cheers.)

Maestro, if you please!

*(Now the Fredericus Rex is played, and three naked girls
are standing on the stage. The first holds a propeller
in her hands, the second a globe and the third a small
zeppelin. Tumultuous applause from the audience, who
jump up from their seats and sing the first verse of
Deutschland Über Alles, after which silence falls.
Gong. The COMPÈRE, in front of the curtain again.)*

And now, ladies and gentlemen, the third tableau:
"The Search for Happiness".

(Deathly silence.)

Maestro, if you please!

*(Schumann's Reverie, and the curtains open for the
third time. A group of naked girls are trampling
each other down, trying to run after a golden sphere,
on which Happiness is balancing on one leg. Happiness
is equally naked and is MARIANNE. VALERIE cries out
shrilly in the dark auditorium.)*

VALERIE: Marianne! Jesus, Mary and Joseph! Marianne!
   (MARIANNE, shocked, starts to wobble on her sphere,
   can't keep her balance, has to step down, and stares,
   blinded by the spotlights, into the dark auditorium.)
AMERICAN: What's the matter?
VALERIE *(beside herself)*: Marianne, Marianne, Marianne!
AMERICAN *(getting furious)*: Will you stop shouting! Are
   you nuts?
VALERIE: Marianne!
AMERICAN: Shut up! I'll give you Marianne!
   (He punches her in the breast. VALERIE screams.
   Uproar in the audience. Shouts of 'Lights! Lights!'
   The COMPÈRE rushes on to the stage.)
COMPÈRE: Curtain! What's going on? Lights! Curtain!
   Lights!
   (The curtain falls in front of MARIANNE, who is still
   staring out into the auditorium, the other girls
   having already exited in confusion. The house-lights
   come up and again, for a moment, there falls a deathly
   hush. Everyone is staring at VALERIE, who is sitting,
   slumped, face down on the table, hysterical and drunk,
   weeping and sobbing. The ZAUBERKÖNIG is standing at
   the bar, his hand on his heart.)
VALERIE *(whimpering)*: Marianne ... Marianne ... dear little
   Marianne ... Oh, oh, oh ... I knew her when she was
   five years old!
COMPÈRE: What's she talking about?
AMERICAN: Search me.
COMPÈRE: Hysterical?
AMERICAN: Epileptic.
A FRIENDLY VOICE: Throw her out, drunken cow!
VALERIE: I'm not drunk. That's one thing I'm not. I'm
   not, I'm not! *(She jumps up, intending to run out,*
86

but trips over her own feet and falls, knocking a
table over as she does so and cutting herself.) I
can't, I can't stand it, I'm not made of stone, I'm
still full of life ... I can't stand it, I can't
stand it!

(She rushes out, bawling. Everyone, except for the
ZAUBERKÖNIG, watches her go, bewildered. Silence,
then the gong. The COMPÈRE gets up on a chair.)

COMPÈRE: Honoured guests! Ladies and gentlemen! That
concludes the official part of tonight's programme ...
the unofficial part is about to commence in the bar!
(Dance music starts up in the bar.)
On behalf of the management, I should like to thank
you for turning up in such numbers and wish you a very
good night. Good night, ladies and gentlemen!
(The clientèle gradually disperses from the club.)

ZAUBERKÖNIG: Captain ...

CAPTAIN: Yes?

ZAUBERKÖNIG: So that's why you wanted to come here instead
of the Moulin Bleu. That was the spicy surprise you
were talking about, I had a funny feeling when you
said that, I had a suspicion it wouldn't be anything
good ...

CAPTAIN: I knew Fräulein Marianne was appearing here. I
come here quite often, I was here yesterday, and I
can't just be a spectator any more. If you weren't
so hard-hearted ...

ZAUBERKÖNIG: Don't interfere in family matters which are
no business of yours, soldier!

CAPTAIN: I considered it my human duty ...

ZAUBERKÖNIG *(interrupting him)*: What's that?

CAPTAIN: You're just not human!

ZAUBERKÖNIG: Oh, that's nice! That's very nice! What am

87

I then, if I'm not human, mm? Perhaps I'm a cow?
Would that suit you? Well, I'm not a cow and I don't
have a daughter either, do you understand?

CAPTAIN: Well, I've nothing more to do here.

(He bows stiffly and exits.)

ZAUBERKÖNIG: And what am I supposed to do here? You
bastard! I feel as if this is the end, Mr. American.
I better write some postcards, so's everyone'll drop
dead with envy, when they hear what a wonderful time
I'm having.

AMERICAN: Postcards! Terrific idea! What an idea!
Postcards!

*(He buys a whole pile from a salesgirl, sits at a
table some way away and starts writing. He's alone
now with the ZAUBERKÖNIG. The sound of dance music
from the bar. MARIANNE enters slowly in a bathrobe
and stops in front of the ZAUBERKÖNIG. The ZAUBER-
KÖNIG stares at her, looks her up and down, then
turns his back on her. Pause.)*

MARIANNE: Why didn't you read my letters? I wrote to
you three times. You sent them back without opening
them.

(Pause.)

I wrote and told you he'd left me ...

*(The ZAUBERKÖNIG turns to her slowly and stares at
her with hatred.)*

ZAUBERKÖNIG: I know that.

(He turns his back on her again. Pause.)

MARIANNE: And did you also know I have a child ...?

ZAUBERKÖNIG: Of course.

(Pause.)

MARIANNE: We're having a hard time, little Leopold and
I ...

88

ZAUBERKÖNIG: What? Leopold? I'm Leopold! This is the limit! Calling your shame after me! On top of everything else! Well, that's the end! You never listened to me, now you'll have to take the consequences. That's the end!
(He gets up, but has to sit down again.)

MARIANNE: You're drunk, Papa ...

ZAUBERKÖNIG: Don't be so vulgar! And once and for all, I'm not your papa! And don't be vulgar, or I'll ... *(He threatens to slap her face.)* You'd do better to think about your mother! The dead see everything!

MARIANNE: If my mother was still alive ...

ZAUBERKÖNIG: You leave your mother out of it, do you hear! If she'd seen you standing around naked on the stage, showing yourself off to everybody ... Have you no shame? My God!

MARIANNE: No, I can't afford shame.
(Silence. The music in the bar has stopped.)
I earn two schillings a day here. It's not much, when you consider little Leopold. But what else is there for me to do? You never let me learn anything, not even eurhythmics, you brought me up to get married ...

ZAUBERKÖNIG: You miserable wretch! Now it's my fault!

MARIANNE: Listen, Papa ...

ZAUBERKÖNIG *(interrupting her)*: I am not your papa!
(MARIANNE bangs the table with her fist.)

MARIANNE: Shut up! If you're not my papa, who is? Now, listen to me, will you? If I lose this job, I've no way of earning anything. I can't go on the game, I can't, I've tried it, but I just can't give myself to a man, unless I love him with all my heart. I'm an uneducated woman, there's nothing else I have to offer ... all that's left for me is the train.

ZAUBERKÖNIG: What train?

MARIANNE: The train. The train you travel on. I'm
   going to throw myself in front of it ...

ZAUBERKÖNIG: I see. That as well. You'd do that to me as
   well. *(He bursts into tears.)* You filthy slut, what
   are you trying to do to my old age? It's one disgrace
   after another. I'm just a poor old man, what have I
   done to deserve this?

MARIANNE *(sharply)*: Stop thinking about yourself the whole
   time!

   *(The ZAUBERKÖNIG stops crying, and stares at her,
   furious.)*

ZAUBERKÖNIG: All right, throw yourself in front of the
   train! Go on, throw yourself in front of it and take
   your brat with you! ... I don't feel well, I don't ...
   I wish I could be sick ... *(He bends forward over the
   table, straightens up suddenly.)* You'd better think
   about God, you'd better think about your Father up
   there in Heaven ...

   *(He staggers off. MARIANNE watches him go then looks
   up towards Heaven.)*

MARIANNE *(quietly)*: In Heaven ...

   *(Dance music starts up again in the bar. The
   AMERICAN has finished writing his postcards and
   notices MARIANNE, who is still looking up to Heaven.)*

AMERICAN: Aha, a dame. *(He watches her, smiling.)* Say, you
   haven't by any chance got a stamp on you?

MARIANNE: No.

AMERICAN *(slowly)*: Only I need two schillings worth of
   stamps and I'm paying fifty schillings for them.
   (Pause.)
   Sixty schillings.
   (Pause. He takes out his wallet.)

90

AMERICAN: Those are the schillings and those are the
   dollars.

MARIANNE: Show me.

   (The AMERICAN hands her the wallet.   Pause.)

MARIANNE: Sixty?

AMERICAN: Sixty-five.

MARIANNE: That's a lot of money.

AMERICAN: It'll be earned.

   (Silence.   The dance music has stopped again.)

MARIANNE: No. Thank you.

   (She gives him back the wallet.)

AMERICAN: What do you mean?

MARIANNE: I can't.   You've made a mistake, sir ...

   (The AMERICAN suddenly grabs her wrist and bellows.)

AMERICAN: Stop! Stop, you've stolen my money, you tart,
   you thief, you criminal, open your hand, open it!

MARIANNE: Ow!

AMERICAN: There!   A hundred schillings!   Did you think I
   wouldn't notice, you stupid whore?   *(He slaps her face.)*
   Police!   Police!

   (Everyone appears from the bar.)

COMPÈRE: For Christ's sake, now what's the matter?

AMERICAN: This whore has stolen my money.   A hundred
   schillings, a hundred schillings!   Police!

   (MARIANNE struggles free from the AMERICAN.)

MARIANNE: You're not to hit me again! I won't be hit again!

   (The BARONESS appears.   MARIANNE cries out in terror.)

II

OUT IN THE WACHAU

*ALFRED sits with his GRANDMOTHER in front of the cottage
in the evening sun. Not far off is the pram.*

GRANDMOTHER: I always knew you were a liar, but I never in
     my wildest dreams realised what a shit you are. You
     borrow three hundred schillings off me to go and work
     for a haulage firm in France, and after three weeks
     you come back and confess you've never even been to
     France, and you've gambled it all away at the races!
     You'll finish up alongside that fine Marianne of yours.
     In gaol!

ALFRED: For one thing she's not in gaol, she's on remand,
     and her trial doesn't come up till tomorrow. Also
     it was only attempted theft, no harm came to anyone,
     there are mitigating circumstances and they're bound
     to give her a suspended sentence, she has no previous
     convictions ...

GRANDMOTHER: That's right, stick up for her, stick up for
     her. You've made a proper fool of me, I knew all
     along you were a criminal.

ALFRED: Won't you forgive me, then?

GRANDMOTHER: Go to hell!

ALFRED: Yah!

     (He sticks his tongue out.)

GRANDMOTHER: Yah!

     (She sticks her tongue out at him. Silence.)

ALFRED *(getting up)*: Well, you won't be seeing me for a
     good long time.

GRANDMOTHER: What about my three hundred schillings? And
     the hundred and fifty I lent you last year?

ALFRED: I don't care how furious it makes you, but to some
    extent I can't help feeling responsible for what's
    happened to Marianne.
    *(GRANDMOTHER gasps for breath. ALFRED raises his
    straw hat.)*
    Enchanté, Granny.
    (He exits.)
GRANDMOTHER *(beside herself with rage)* And mind you don't
    come back! Mucky bastard! How dare you speak to me like
    that? Go on, get out of here, you shit!
    *(She sits at the table on which her zither is lying
    and tunes it. ALFRED's MOTHER comes out of the
    cottage.)*
MOTHER: Has Alfred gone already?
GRANDMOTHER: Yes, thank God!
MOTHER: He didn't even say good-bye ...
GRANDMOTHER: That's a fine son you've got there, insolent
    and idle! Just like his father.
MOTHER: Leave my husband alone! He's been in his grave
    ten years now and you still won't leave him alone.
GRANDMOTHER: Yes, and what put him in his grave so soon,
    I'd like to know. Me, I suppose? Or was it his
    precious alcohol? He pissed away your whole dowry.
MOTHER: I don't want to hear any more, that's enough!
GRANDMOTHER: Then shut up!
    (She plays the Doppeladler March *on her zither.
    MOTHER bends anxiously over the pram and GRANDMOTHER
    ends her march.)*
MOTHER: I'm worried about Leopold, he's got such a bad
    cough, and now his cheeks are all red and he looks
    quite different ... just like the way it started
    with poor little Ludwig ...
GRANDMOTHER: The Lord giveth and the Lord taketh away.

MOTHER: Mama!

GRANDMOTHER: Its mother in gaol and its father a layabout. It'd be better for a lot of people if it wasn't here any more.

MOTHER: How would you like it if you weren't here any more?

GRANDMOTHER *(shrieking)*: Don't you compare me with that thing! *(She points at the pram.)* My parents were decent people!

(She plays a minuet, furious.)

MOTHER: Will you stop that!

GRANDMOTHER: There's no need to shout! Have you gone mad?

(They stare at one another. Silence.)

MOTHER *(frightened)*: Mama ... I saw you ...

GRANDMOTHER: What?

MOTHER: I saw you last night ...

(Silence.)

GRANDMOTHER *(warily)*: What do you mean?

MOTHER: You opened both the windows and moved Leopold's cot into the draught.

GRANDMOTHER *(shrieking)*: You dreamt it! You dreamt it!

MOTHER: No, I didn't dream it. And I don't care how furious you get.

III

AND ONCE AGAIN IN THE QUIET STREET IN VIENNA 8

The CAPTAIN is reading the list of lottery results again and VALERIE is standing in the doorway of her tobacconist's. Everything seems the same as ever, except that in the window of the dolls' hospital, there's a sign saying: 'Clearance Sale'.

VALERIE *(maliciously)*: And what have we won then, captain?
    (The CAPTAIN hands her back the list.)

CAPTAIN: It's Saturday, Frau Valerie. And tomorrow's
    Sunday.

VALERIE: That's life, captain, that's the human condition.

CAPTAIN: Clearance sale! My conscience is clear, but
    all the same. My motives were entirely altruistic that
    time in Maxim's. A reconciliation was what I wanted,
    a reconciliation. And because of that, it's just been
    one tragedy after another. Poor Marianne locked up
    and sentenced ...

VALERIE *(interrupting him)*: Only a suspended sentence,
    captain.
    (Silence.)

CAPTAIN: Is he really still angry with me, Herr Zauberkönig?

VALERIE: Why should he be?

CAPTAIN: Well, I mean, because of the terrible position
    I put him in at Maxim's.

VALERIE: But, captain, after all the things that man's
    been through, he doesn't want to be angry with you any
    more. He's got much more forgiving, he's a broken
    man. The other day, when he heard Marianne was a
    thief, he practically had a stroke!

CAPTAIN: It's no joke, a heart attack.

VALERIE: He heard the music of the spheres.

CAPTAIN: What do you mean, the music of the spheres?

VALERIE: When someone's very close to death, the soul
    starts to leave the body, only half the soul, I mean,
    and it flies away, up higher and higher, and up there
    there's a strange melody playing, and that's the music
    of the spheres.
    (Silence.)

CAPTAIN: I suppose it's possible. Theoretically.

*(The schoolgirl on the second floor starts to play a
Johann Strauss waltz.)*

VALERIE: Can you keep a secret, captain?

CAPTAIN: Of course!

VALERIE: Promise?

CAPTAIN: Well, I should think an old officer could keep a
secret. Just think of all the military secrets I
know!

(Pause.)

VALERIE: Captain. She's been to see me.

CAPTAIN: Who?

VALERIE: Marianne. That's right, Marianne. She came
looking for me. Four weeks she'd been in custody
and she had nothing left but her pride, although she
still had that. Until I got rid of it for her, that
is, and I can tell you, I got rid of it all right.
Just leave it to me, captain, I'll get her and her
papa back together again, we women understand how to
fix these things much better than men. What you
tried to do in Maxim's was much too direct ... my
God, it gave me a fright, I can tell you!

CAPTAIN: All's well that ends well.

*(ERICH enters quickly, right. He's on his way to the
dolls' hospital, but spots the CAPTAIN and glares at
him. The schoolgirl breaks off the waltz in mid-
phrase. The CAPTAIN looks contemptuously at ERICH,
then bows politely to VALERIE and exits, passing
close by ERICH. ERICH watches him go, balefully,
then looks at VALERIE. VALERIE starts to exit into
the tobacconist's.)*

ERICH: Wait! One moment, dear lady. I just wanted to
draw your attention to the fact that we shall probably
never see each other again ...

96

VALERIE: Good!

ERICH: I'm leaving first thing tomorrow. For ever.

VALERIE: Bon voyage!

ERICH: Thank you.

> *(He bows formally, then starts off towards the dolls'*
> *hospital.)*

VALERIE *(suddenly)*: Stop!

ERICH: As you were!

> *(Silence.)*

VALERIE: We ought not to say good-bye like this. Come
on, let's shake hands. Let's part good friends.

ERICH: All right. *(He shakes hands with her, then takes*
a notebook out of his pocket and leafs through it.)
It's all down in black and white. Debit and credit.
Every single cigarette.

VALERIE *(amiably)*: I don't want your cigarettes ...

ERICH: It's a matter of honour!

> *(VALERIE takes the hand holding the notebook and*
> *strokes it.)*

VALERIE: You're no psychologist, Erich ...

> *(She gives him a friendly nod and slowly exits into*
> *the tobacconist's. The schoolgirl starts playing*
> *again. ERICH watches her go. He's alone.)*

ERICH: Fifty-year-old decaying piece of shit ...

> *(He exits into the dolls' hospital. OSKAR comes out*
> *of the butcher's with ALFRED.)*

OSKAR: Well, in any case, thanks very much for coming to
see me ... and for being so agreeable apropos Marianne.

ALFRED: Just let's leave it at that. I renounce all
claims on her. For good. *(He notices the sign in the*
window of the dolls' hospital.) What's that?
Clearance sale?

OSKAR *(smiles)*: Yes, that as well, my friend. Soon

there'll be no magic round here any more, that's to
say, unless there's a reconciliation with our
Marianne, because the old man just can't manage it on
his own any more ...

ALFRED: How sad it all is. Believe me, it's really not
my fault, everything that's happened. When I think
about it now, I can't understand it, I had it so good
in those days, no problems, no worries. And then to
be so careless as to let myself get mixed up in an
adventure like that. It serves me right, God knows
what got into me!

OSKAR: I think it was true love.

ALFRED: Oh no, I've got no talent for that. I was too
kind-hearted, that's all. I just can't say no, and if
you can't say no, a relationship like that's automatically going to go from bad to worse. You see, at
the time, I really didn't want to break up your
engagement, but with a girl like Marianne, it's got to
be all or nothing, she insisted. You understand what
I mean?

OSKAR: Of course. It's only on the surface the man seems
to play the active part and the woman the passive. If
you look into it a bit more closely ...

ALFRED: You can see the abyss opening.

OSKAR: See, that's why I never really had anything against
you personally, I never wished you any harm ... whereas
Marianne ... *(He smiles.)* she's had to pay a bitter
price, all right, poor thing, for the grand passion of
her life ...

ALFRED: Making so many people unhappy like that, it's
terrible. Honestly, we men ought to stick together
more.

OSKAR: We're too naive, if you ask me.
98

ALFRED: You said it.

(The schoolgirl breaks off again.)

Oskar, I don't know how to thank you for promising to
help me and Valerie get back together again ...

OSKAR *(interrupting him)*: Ssh!

*(The ZAUBERKÖNIG comes out of the dolls' hospital with
ERICH. Neither of them notices ALFRED or OSKAR, who
draw back into the doorway of the butcher's.)*

ZAUBERKÖNIG: Don't forget, have a good trip, Erich! Take
care and safe journey to Dessau!

ERICH: Kassel, Uncle.

ZAUBERKÖNIG: Kassel, Dessau, I'll never learn. And don't
forget our Vienna and your poor old uncle!

*(ERICH clicks his heels again, bows stiffly and exits
without looking back. The ZAUBERKÖNIG watches him go,
moved, then notices VALERIE, who, hearing ERICH's
voice, has appeared in her doorway again to listen.)*

One of the best, eh?

*(The schoolgirl starts playing again. VALERIE slowly
nods in agreement. The ZAUBERKÖNIG picks up a newspaper from the rack in front of the tobacconist's
and leafs through it.)*

Yes, Yes, Europe has to unite, because the next
war'll be the end of all of us. But how are we
supposed to put up with all this? I mean, what do
the Czechs think they're up to? I'm telling you
now: very soon there's going to be another war. There
just has to be! There'll always be wars.

VALERIE *(still elsewhere)*: True. But that would mean
the end of our civilisation as we know it.

ZAUBERKÖNIG: Civilisation or no civilisation, war's a law
of nature. Just like competition in business. I
mean, personally, I've got no competition, because I'm

99

a specialised trade. And even so, I'm ruined. I
just can't manage on my own any more, every customer
I get makes me nervous. Before, I had my wife, and
when she started to get ill, Marianne was already old
enough ...

VALERIE: How old?

ZAUBERKÖNIG: Old enough!

(Pause.)

VALERIE: If I were a grandfather ...

ZAUBERKÖNIG *(interrupting her)*: But I'm not a grandfather,
if you don't mind! *(He clutches his heart. The
waltz breaks off.)* You mustn't get me excited! Ow,
my heart ...

(Silence.)

VALERIE: Does it hurt?

ZAUBERKÖNIG: Like hell. And you know what the doctor
said. I could have a heart attack just like that.

VALERIE: I remember that from my poor husband. Shooting
pains, is it?

ZAUBERKÖNIG: Shooting pains, that's right ...

(Silence.)

VALERIE: Leopold. God has given you a sign. And what it
is is that you're still alive. Now, calm down, don't
get excited, don't get excited! Otherwise you'll have
a heart attack, and if you have a heart attack, then
what? You silly old buffer, the best thing to do is
forgive and forget. Forgive and forget, and you'll
be able to carry on your business and everything will
be all right, everything, everything!

(Silence.)

ZAUBERKÖNIG: You think so?

VALERIE: Look, Marianne, she's not a bad person, she's
just a stupid little woman. Just a poor stupid

little woman.

ZAUBERKÖNIG: She's stupid all right. Thick as pigshit.

VALERIE: And she thought she could change the world the
way she wanted it to be. But I'm afraid the world
behaves according to reason, isn't that right, Grandpa?

ZAUBERKÖNIG: Grandpa?

VALERIE: Yes.

> *(Silence. The schoolgirl starts playing again. The
> ZAUBERKÖNIG moves off slowly towards the dolls'
> hospital, stops in front of the window and looks at
> the clearance sale sign. Then he gives VALERIE a
> friendly nod, tears up the sign and vanishes into the
> dolls' hospital. VALERIE grins with satisfaction and
> lights a cigarette.)*

OSKAR: Frau Valerie! I have a surprise for you.

VALERIE: What sort of a surprise?

OSKAR: Someone wants to make it up with you.

VALERIE: Who? Erich?

OSKAR: No.

VALERIE: Then who?

OSKAR: Him.

> *(VALERIE approaches the butcher's and sees ALFRED.
> ALFRED bows. Pause.)*

VALERIE: Oh.

> *(The music has stopped again.)*

ALFRED: You've no idea the inner struggles this has cost
me, coming to eat humble pie like this. But I'm not
ashamed to do it any more, because I know I treated
you badly.

VALERIE: Me?

ALFRED: Yes.

VALERIE: When was that, then?

> *(ALFRED is puzzled.)*

VALERIE: You've never done me any harm.

(ALFRED is even more puzzled. He smiles, embarrassed.)

ALFRED: Well, after all, I did leave you ...

VALERIE: You left me? I left you! Anyway, there was no
    harm in that, it was a very good thing, and don't you
    forget it, you vain monkey!

ALFRED: We parted good friends, though, didn't we?

VALERIE: We parted, didn't we, and that was that! I'm
    not going to have anything more to do with a complete
    swine!

(Silence.)

ALFRED: What do you mean, a complete swine? You just said
    I didn't do you any harm!

VALERIE: I'm not talking about me! I'm talking about
    Marianne! And your baby!

(Silence.)

ALFRED: Marianne always said I must be a hypnotist ... *(He
    shouts at her.)* Is it my fault I have such a powerful
    effect on women?

VALERIE: Don't you shout at me!

OSKAR: In my opinion, I mean, relatively speaking, Alfred
    was rather good to Marianne.

VALERIE: You men, always helping each other out! I have
    my share of female solidarity as well, you know. *(To
    ALFRED.)* I'd like to see you cut down to size, really
    cut down to size!

(Silence.)

ALFRED: I've been routed. You don't have to tell me twice
    I'm a bad person, I know it, and the reason is, when
    it really comes down to it, I'm weak. I've always
    needed someone to look after, I have to have it,
    otherwise I'm lost. But I just couldn't look after
    Marianne, that was just my bad luck ... I mean, if I'd

102

still had some capital, I could have played the
horses, except she wouldn't let me ...

VALERIE: She wouldn't let you?

ALFRED: She thought it was immoral.

VALERIE: That was stupid of her, it's the only thing
you're any good at.

ALFRED: You see! And that's the only reason our relationship finally fell to pieces, different way of
looking at things. It was quite spontaneous.

VALERIE: You're a liar.

(Silence.)

ALFRED: Valerie. I sold skin cream, I sold fountain
pens, I sold Persian carpets ... The whole thing was
a disaster, and now I'm really in a bloody awful
situation. You used to be so understanding about
other people's complications ...

VALERIE *(interrupting him)*: How was France?

ALFRED: Much the same as here.

VALERIE: And how were the French girls?

ALFRED: Same as they all are. Ungrateful.

VALERIE *(smiles)*: You bugger. What would you do, if I
was to lend you fifty schillings?

(Silence.)

ALFRED: Fifty?

VALERIE: Yes.

ALFRED: Well, of course, I'd send it straight off to
Maisons-Laffitte, win or a place ...

VALERIE *(interrupting him)*: And then what?

ALFRED: How do you mean?

VALERIE: What would you do with the winnings?

(Silence.)

ALFRED *(cunning smile)*: The money I'd be likely to win, I'd
hand over personally to my son tomorrow ...

VALERIE: I'll believe that when I see it!

(MARIANNE enters quickly and stops, frightened.)

OSKAR: Marianne!

VALERIE: Well, well!

(MARIANNE looks from one to the other and starts to leave, quickly.)

Wait! Don't go! It's time we cleared up this mess, it's spring-cleaning time. It's time to make things up once and for all!

(Silence.)

OSKAR: Marianne. I'm quite prepared to forgive you for everything you've done to me, because loving someone brings you more happiness than being loved. If you have a shred of feeling left in you, you must know that in spite of everything, I'd take you to the altar today, that is if you were still free, what I mean is, the child ...

(Silence.)

MARIANNE: What are you talking about?

OSKAR *(smiles)*: I'm sorry.

MARIANNE: What about?

OSKAR: The child ...

(Silence.)

MARIANNE: Leave the baby out of it, will you? What's the baby done to you? And don't look at me in that stupid way!

VALERIE: Marianne! This is supposed to be a reconciliation.

MARIANNE *(pointing at ALFRED)*: Not with him!

VALERIE: Him as well. All or nothing. After all, he's only a human being!

ALFRED: Thanks very much.

MARIANNE: Yesterday you said he was a mean-minded animal.

VALERIE: Yesterday was yesterday, and today's today, and

anyway you mind your own business.

ALFRED: He who loves change alone will be my friend.

OSKAR *(to MARIANNE)*:

> If you love not in your heart
>
> Death and resurrection,
>
> You can only be a part
>
> Of the world's infection.

MARIANNE *(grins)*: My God, you're educated.

OSKAR: Got it off a calendar.

VALERIE: Calendar or no calendar, he's only a human being after all, with all the inborn failings and vices. You just didn't give him the kind of stability he needs.

MARIANNE: I did my best!

VALERIE: You're just too young!

> *(Silence.)*

ALFRED: When it comes down to it, I was no angel either.

VALERIE: When it comes down to it, it's really no-one's fault, that kind of a liaison. When it really comes down to it, it's all a question of the stars, some aura attracting us to each other and all that.

MARIANNE: But they locked me up.

> *(Silence.)*
>
> They really humiliated me.

OSKAR: Well, you can't expect the police to wear kid gloves.

VALERIE: At least they were women officers, weren't they?

MARIANNE: Some of them.

VALERIE: Well, then!

> *(Silence.)*
>
> Marianne, dear. What you must do now, is just go quietly in there ...
>
> *(She points to the dolls' hospital.)*

MARIANNE: Why?

VALERIE: Just go ...

MARIANNE: All right, it's your responsibility.

VALERIE: My responsibility.

> *(Silence. MARIANNE turns slowly towards the dolls'*
> *hospital, puts her hand on the door-knob, then turns*
> *back to VALERIE, ALFRED and OSKAR.)*

MARIANNE: I just want to say one thing. When it really comes
down to it, I don't give a shit. What I'm doing, I'm doing
for Leopold, because none of this is his fault ...

> *(She opens the door, and the peal of bells rings out,*
> *as if nothing had happened.)*

IV

OUT IN THE WACHAU

ALFRED's GRANDMOTHER is sitting in the sun and his MOTHER
is peeling potatoes. And the pram is nowhere to be seen.

GRANDMOTHER: Frieda! Have you written the letter?

MOTHER: No.

GRANDMOTHER: Do you want me to write it?

> *(Silence.)*

Since Alfred hasn't given us his address, we've got
to write to her ...

MOTHER: I'll do it, I'll do it. They'll blame us for not
being more careful ...

GRANDMOTHER: Us? You! You, you mean.

MOTHER: It wasn't my fault.

GRANDMOTHER: I suppose it was my idea, taking the baby?
Well, it wasn't, it was your idea, because you wanted
a sweet little thing in the house, that's what you said.
I was always against it. That kind of thing, it's

nothing but trouble.

MOTHER: All right. It's my fault as usual. All right.
And I suppose it was my fault little Leopold caught
cold as well and went to Heaven? My God, it's all
so terrible!

(Silence.)

GRANDMOTHER: Maybe it's not as terrible as all that. I'm
thinking about your Fräulein Marianne. You know what
they are, those girls. Perhaps she'll be quite
pleased to be rid of it ...

MOTHER: Mama! Are you mad?

GRANDMOTHER: What are you talking about, you stupid cow?

MOTHER: What are you talking about, you monster? She is
a mother, after all, just the same as you!

GRANDMOTHER *(shrieking)*: Don't you compare me with her!
My child was born in wedlock, or perhaps you think
you're a bastard? When there's no blessing from
above, it always ends badly and so it should! Otherwise where would we be? Now it's time that letter was
written, and if you're too scared to do it, I'll
dictate it to you. *(She gets up.)* Sit down here.
There's pencil and paper there. I've got it all ready.

MOTHER: Monster ...

GRANDMOTHER: Shut up! Sit down! Write! Be thankful I'm
helping you!

*(The MOTHER sits down. The GRANDMOTHER walks up and
down, hunched up, and dictates.)*

Dear Fräulein. That's right, Fräulein! I'm afraid
we have to inform you of a very sad piece of news for
you. In his inscrutable wisdom, Almighty God has
decreed, that you, dear Fräulein, no longer have a
child. It was only a little cold, but the child passed
away very quickly. Full stop. But you must be of

107

good cheer, because Almighty God loves innocent
children. Full stop. New paragraph.

*(MARIANNE enters, with the ZAUBERKÖNIG, VALERIE, OSKAR
and ALFRED. She has hurried on a little ahead of them.)*

MARIANNE: Hello, Frau Zentner. Nice to see you, Grand-
mama! I know I haven't been here for some time, but
I'm very pleased to see you again. This is my father.

(The ZAUBERKÖNIG bows.)

MOTHER *(noticing ALFRED)*: Alfred!

MARIANNE *(suddenly uneasy)*: What's the matter ...?

*(The GRANDMOTHER hands her the letter. She takes
it mechanically and looks around timidly.)*

(Frightened) Where is he ...? Where is he ...?

GRANDMOTHER: Read it, please. Just read it.

(MARIANNE reads the letter.)

ZAUBERKÖNIG: Well, where's little Leopold, then?

*(He is holding a toy in his hand, with bells attached
to it. He jingles it.)*

Grandpa's here! It's grandpa!

(MARIANNE drops the letter. Silence.)

(Suddenly anxious) Marianne! Is something the matter?

(VALERIE has picked up the letter and read it.)

VALERIE *(crying out)*: Mother of God! He's dead! Little
Leopold's gone!

ALFRED: Dead?

VALERIE: Dead!

*(She sobs. ALFRED automatically puts his arms round
her. The ZAUBERKÖNIG staggers. He drops the toy and
buries his face in his hands. Silence. The GRAND-
MOTHER picks up the toy, curious, and jingles it.
MARIANNE watches her; then suddenly throws herself
silently at her and tries to kill her with the zither,
which is lying on the table. OSKAR grabs her round*

108

           the throat. MARIANNE chokes and drops the zither.
           Silence. The GRANDMOTHER picks up the zither.)

GRANDMOTHER *(quietly)*: You bitch. You pig. You gaolbird.
    You'd like to kill me, would you? Would you?
MOTHER *(suddenly shouting at the GRANDMOTHER)*: You get
    back in the house, go on, hurry up!
    (The GRANDMOTHER comes up to the MOTHER slowly.)
GRANDMOTHER: That'd just suit you, wouldn't it, if I were
    in my grave, that's what you've been wanting for ages,
    isn't it? But I'm not going yet awhile, I'm not
    going yet. See? *(She slaps the MOTHER's face.)*
    Well, those of you who want me to die, I hope you
    all rot!
    (She exits into the cottage with her zither. Silence.)
MOTHER *(sobbing)*: You'll be sorry for that!
    *(She follows her in. The ZAUBERKÖNIG slowly takes his
    hands away from his face.)*
ZAUBERKÖNIG: Another heart attack, another heart attack ...
    dear God, no, no, no, give me a little more time, God.
    (He crosses himself.) Our Father, which art in
    Heaven ... God is great, God is just ... you are
    just, God, aren't you? Give me a little more time,
    just a little. You are just, you are just!
    (He straightens his tie and exits slowly.)
VALERIE *(to ALFRED)*: How old was he, little Leopold?
ALFRED: Not very old.
VALERIE: My most sincere condolences.
ALFRED: Thank you. *(He takes some banknotes out of his
    trouser pocket.)* Look. I sent off to Maisons-Laffitte
    yesterday and won. And today I wanted to give my son
    eighty-four schillings ...
VALERIE: We'll buy him a nice tombstone. A praying angel,
    something along those lines.

                                                        109

ALFRED: I'm very sad. I really am. I was just thinking,
    just now, without children, you're really nothing.
    There's no continuity, you just become extinct. What
    a shame!

    (He exits slowly with VALERIE.)

MARIANNE: I once asked God what was to become of me. He
    didn't tell me, otherwise I wouldn't be here any
    more. He didn't tell me anything. He wanted it to
    be a surprise. Damn Him!

OSKAR: Marianne! Never quarrel with God!

MARIANNE: Damn Him! Damn Him!

    (She spits. Silence.)

OSKAR: Marianne. God knows what He's doing, believe me!

MARIANNE: Where's my baby? Where are you? Where?

OSKAR: He's in Paradise.

MARIANNE: There's no need to torment me ...

OSKAR: I'm not a sadist. I'm only trying to comfort you.
    Your whole life still lies ahead of you. This is just
    the beginning. The Lord giveth and the Lord taketh
    away.

MARIANNE: He's done nothing but take away from me, nothing.

OSKAR: God is love, Marianne. And whom the Lord loveth,
    He chasteneth ...

MARIANNE: He's beaten me like a dog!

OSKAR: Well, if it has to be, it has to be.

    *(Inside the cottage, the GRANDMOTHER starts playing
    Johann Strauss's* Tales From The Vienna Woods *on her
    zither.)*

    Marianne. I once told you I hoped you'd never have to
    go through what you made me suffer. And even now God
    has left you people who love you in spite of everything.
    And now everything's been put right like this ... I
    once told you, Marianne, you wouldn't escape my love ...

110

MARIANNE: I'm finished. I'm finished now ...

OSKAR: Come along, then ...

> *(He supports her, kisses her on the mouth and slowly*
> *exits with her. And there's a humming and ringing in*
> *the air, as if some heavenly string orchestra were*
> *playing the* Tales From the Vienna Woods *by Johann*
> *Strauss.)*

Songs

Act I Scene 3 (page 33)

'Sei gepriesen, du lauschige Nacht ...'

Glory be to that heavenly night,
When two young hearts their troth did plight.
Next year the altar-rose espied
The couple kneeling side by side!
And Mr. Stork soon left his nest
And flew to their home with a bundle blest.
Although sweet May once again disappeared,
When you're young at heart it blooms every year.

'Es kam einst gezogen ein Bursch ganz allein ...'

A happy young wanderer all by himself
Came sauntering along once as evening fell.
It was then he encountered a glance and a smile
That would live in his memory a very long while.
Her cheeks were so rosy, her eyes were so bright,
Her hair was so golden, her face a delight.
The girl he had seen there long haunted his brain
And often he sang to himself this refrain:

    Way out there in the Wachau
    The Danube flows so blue,
    In a cottage among the vines,
    Her face at the window shines.
    Her lips are red as blood,
    Her kisses taste so good,
    Her eyes are violet blue,
    The girl out in the Wachau.

'Da draussen in der Wachau ...'

Way out there in the Wachau
The Danube flows so blue,
In a cottage among the vines,
Her face at the window shines.
Her lips are red as blood,
Her kisses taste so good,
Her eyes are violet blue,
The girl out in the Wachau.

'Es wird ein Wein sein ...'

There will be wines to drink
We won't be here to drink
And girls to smile upon
When we are dead and gone ...

'Drum gehn wir gern nach Nussdorf naus ...'

So off we go to old Nussdorf
To have some fun and games
And dance the night away
And hear the handsome yodellers sing
And in the wee small hours
Go staggering home, go staggering home!

Act III Scene 1 (page 76)

'Ach, ich hab sie jar nur ...'

Oh, a kiss on the shoulder was all that I tried ...
and the next thing was I felt the slap of her fan
upon my cheek.

Act III Scene 1 (page 79)

'Mein Muatterl war a Wienerin ...'

My mother was from Vienna,
That's why I love it so,
With a love that I knew
From the first breath I drew
For this golden Vienna of mine!

'Wien, Wien, nur du allein ...'

Vienna, you alone
Will be the city I call my own,
City of laughter and dreams come true
Vienna, I love you!

Act III Scene 1 (page 80)

'Mir ist mei Alte gstorbn ...'

Oh, my old lady's dead
And I still feel the pain.
Such a kind-hearted soul
I'll never find again.
I can't help crying.
Don't think I'm lying
It makes me so upset
When I think of my old pet! Olé!

'Vindobona, du herrliche Stadt ...'

Vindobona, you beautiful city,
All your walks and parks are so pretty,
You will always live in our heart
And draw us to you when we're apart.
Where'er we wander, far or near,
We'll never forget our Vienna's here.
You'll always be old Austria's pearl,
The loveliest city in all the world!

Now Mizzi and her Jean
Go walking arm in arm,
We're not made out of stone,
We're young and full of go,
It's not jam every day,
But we're going to make hay,
Today we're going to 'Brady's'
Or 'Maxim's' for the ladies!

Let's crack another bottle of wine,
Hollodero!
And it won't be the last in line,
Hollodero!
And if it is, so what, says I
Hollodero!
We're going to sing it one more time, let's
    sing it one more time!